Getting Things Done and Stop Wasting Time

Beat the Procrastination Equation with the Highly Effective Cure Boosting Productivity and Daily Self-Discipline

Paul B. Heathcote

© Copyright 2019 - All rights reserved.

The content contained within this book may not be reproduced, duplicated or transmitted without direct written permission from the author or the publisher.

Under no circumstances will any blame or legal responsibility be held against the publisher, or author, for any damages, reparation, or monetary loss due to the information contained within this book. Either directly or indirectly.

Legal Notice

This book is copyright protected. This book is only for personal use. You cannot amend, distribute, sell, use, quote or paraphrase any part, or the content within this book, without the consent of the author or publisher.

Disclaimer Notice

Please note the information contained within this document is for educational and entertainment purposes only. All effort has been executed to present accurate, up to date, and reliable, complete information. No warranties of any kind are declared or implied. Readers acknowledge that the author is not engaging in the rendering of legal, financial, medical or professional advice. The content within this book has been derived from various sources. Please consult a licensed professional before attempting any techniques outlined in this book.

By reading this document, the reader agrees that under no circumstances is the author responsible for any losses, direct or indirect, which are incurred as a result of the use of information contained within this document, including, but not limited to, — errors, omissions, or inaccuracies.

Contents

Chapter 1:
Why Do I Procrastinate? Is It Really A Problem? _____ 1

Chapter 2:
The Willingness to Accept Change _____ 10

Chapter 3:
Dealing with Setbacks and Bad Habits _____ 18

Chapter 4:
Why Waiting for Tomorrow Is A Bad Idea _____ 26

Chapter 5:
The Power to Start (5 Second Rule) _____ 34

Chapter 6:
Eat That Frog _____ 45

Chapter 7:
Stop Filling the Void with Meaningless Tasks _____ 53

Chapter 8:
Your Environment Is Unproductive _____ 63

Chapter 9:
Think Optimistically _____ 70

Chapter 10:
Tunnel Vision Is Great _____ 79

Chapter 11:
Kaizen to Overcome Laziness _____ 88

Chapter 12:
There Is No Shame in Rewarding Yourself_____ 96

Chapter 13:
Time Chunking Never Fails _____ 101

Chapter 14:
Stop Sabotaging Yourself (Manage Procrastination) _____ 110

Chapter 15:
7 Steps to Stop Procrastinating _____ 115

Chapter 16:
Stop Wasting Time on The Internet _____ 125

Chapter 1:
Why Do I Procrastinate? Is It Really A Problem?

Everyone hates it when they have something to do, but don't want to do it or lack the motivation to get started. Procrastination affects almost everyone at some point in life. However, some people procrastinate so much that they continually avoid obligations that they hate, resulting in negative emotions that have very adverse effects.

You should not allow procrastination to rule your life. By having the right knowledge about procrastination, you can beat it and gain inner focus and motivation. For you to stop procrastination from impacting your life, you should understand the reason or reasons that you are falling victim to it. In this chapter, you will discover the leading causes of procrastination, and you should note the specific causes that are most relevant to you. Try to determine which arguments resonate with you.

By doing this, you will gain the knowledge that you can use to overcome procrastination. Knowing more about what makes you procrastinate will help you defeat this monster. Just as you can fight disease when you know its causes, or battle a known enemy, in the same way it will be easy to stop procrastinating after learning what is causing it.

Without further ado, let us look at the possible reasons you are procrastinating:

Believing That You Must Be Motivated Before Acting

Do you often find yourself saying things like, "I don't feel like doing this assignment," or "I don't feel like waking up"? This may be a sign that you lack motivation. This is the main reason why most people avoid doing unpleasant tasks. Most victims of procrastination believe that there is something wrong with them if they are not motivated to start a certain task. However, this is not true. Imagine how many people wake up early in the morning and do unpleasant tasks yet never quit. Numberless people do unpleasant and unmotivating tasks each day and, guess what, they don't procrastinate. There may be no motivation in cleaning a car, or even cleaning your boss's office, but you still find some people succeeding in accomplishing these tasks without procrastinating.

Therefore, believing that you should feel motivated in order to act does not work for you, but against you. One thing that I have realized over time is that acting should come first. Starting an assignment or a task is the real motivator, instead of waiting to feel motivated before beginning to take steps. You will be surprised that after you take the first step, no matter how insignificant it may seem, you will be encouraged and eventually motivated to take further steps.

If your motivation is really standing in your way and making you procrastinate, you should analyze your attitude and determine whether it is preventing you from becoming motivated. If you find that your attitude is preventing you from becoming motivated, find a way to adjust it. You can do this by changing your mindset from thinking that everything in your life should be exciting, or that you must like your assignments for you to value them. Sometimes what we desire does not align with our broader goals, so you should learn how to control your mindset and avoid procrastinating on things simply because you don't like them. Re-evaluate and understand the steps that will lead to your final goal. If you discover that being in places that you don't like or doing boring things are necessary to attain your larger goals, that alone should motivate you to act.

Fear of Failure

Do you fear failure? If you answered yes, the chances are high that you are a procrastinator. When your mind is so conscious of failure, you will find yourself arguing that if you do your best and still fail, it will be worse than if you didn't try at all. Procrastinators don't like putting in the effort and failing and will even argue that if they did not try at all, they didn't technically fail. For instance, you may have an exam in your class. One person may decide to do their best in studying and reviewing the material, whereas a procrastinator will either not study or wait until the night before the exam. When the results of the exam are out, and the procrastinator did not do well, he will argue that he has not truly failed because if he had studied more, the results would have been better.

Imagine that you are supposed to do research for a project, but due to procrastination, you wait until it is too late before starting your research. The result of this will be a poorly researched project that will not meet the set requirements. You will comfort yourself by saying that you would have done better if you had given it the required time.

Here, the reason for procrastinating is so you can protect yourself from the reality of "real" failure. Since you didn't put all the necessary effort into your work, you don't realize your true capabilities. Procrastinators avoid doing the most important tasks by filling their schedule with busy work, so they appear to have "good" reasons for not doing them.

The fear of failure is a real thing and can cause you to put aside your important obligations until another day. Your success in work, school, sports, or any other area of your life is dependent on how your mindset regarding your talents and abilities. Some people have a mindset geared towards growth, whereas others have a fixed mindset. Those who have a fixed mindset believe that nothing more can be done to improve their current abilities. These people also argue that, if you have talent, no effort is required for you to succeed. According to them, talent comes naturally. However, this is a very dangerous mindset because it hinders your ability to learn, grow, and make fruitful changes.

On the other hand, when a person has mindset geared towards growth, they will believe that their abilities can be improved through hard work and dedication. Your brain and talents are only a starting point but are not the limit to what you can achieve. By confining yourself to your current talents and abilities, you will feel more comfortable avoiding the things that you are not good at. Eventually, this will make you procrastinate due to the fear of making mistakes.

Thinking That You Can Do It Later

This is a common excuse for many people: always assuming you can work on your pending task later. Do you ever find yourself thinking that in a couple of hours or days, you will be in a better place to handle a task? This is a sign of procrastination. You should understand that you have little control of the future, and postponing responsibilities could mean that you will never accomplish some of those tasks at all. You have no control over the future because your mood or state of mind may worsen compared to your present state, which might prevent you from doing the task in the time that you thought you could.

You should also be aware that decision-making preferences vary over time, meaning different aspects of you could be more dominant when making decisions at different times. When those preferences are unaligned, there will be inconsistency. Again, you can't ignore the factor of unpredictability. For instance, a day before a scheduled assignment or exam, the participants wish they could have two more days to do more research. If allowed, the participants would pay any amount for that assignment or exam to be postponed for even for a day. Surprisingly, if they were asked the same question three or four weeks before, very few participants would feel the need to change the assignment date. And no one would be willing to pay any amount, no matter how small, to change the date.

Although the participants are faced with the same choice both times, each decision is made at a different point in time and generates a different reaction. The change in the decision of the participants is due to the time inconsistency. This means that people's minds change over time, which can strongly impact their decisions. We often think differently and make different decisions about what will affect us soon as opposed to what will affect us in the long term.

Therefore, postponing your assignment until a later date might mean that you will never do it. This will cause you to fail in achieving some of your most important goals as a result of procrastination.

Unsure of How to Begin

One of the reasons that you procrastinate is because you have a complex task that you find challenging even to start. Not knowing the first step in handling a task can be daunting. Sometimes you might be lucky enough to know the first step, but you discover that you miscalculated how much time and commitment would be required to complete it, leading to procrastination.

Feeling Bored by A Task

We all lack interest in doing some important things in our life from time to time. However, that does not mean that we should procrastinate over them. For example, many students complain that they lack interest in a course that they are taking. This does not mean that they should stop studying. Our level of interest should not control what we do or don't do, because it can make us fail to achieve some of our goals.

Procrastination works against our success. Therefore, it is best to make the right decisions even if it means doing something that we are not fully interested in. Keep in mind the benefits that you will gain after committing yourself to action. Even though it may not align with your interests, it will help you avoid procrastination and keep moving. Even if you are not interested in that career or that course, you should try it. It may not be easy, but it is the best way to avoid procrastinating and to advance in life. If you give in to procrastination, you will never achieve your goals and may end up losing interest in life in general.

Skills Deficit

Lacking the necessary skills to do specific tasks can make you procrastinate. In this case, you procrastinate because you don't want to admit that you lack the needed skills. It is common for any person to lack certain skills, but not all procrastinate; some own up to their lack of knowledge in that area and try to learn. However, for procrastinators, they will find it challenging to admit to their lack of skill and, instead, opt to procrastinate.

We all face a deficit in certain skills, but you should not think that you yourself are dumb or lacking just because you aren't familiar with performing certain tasks. This is an attitude that can cost you your success. Don't embrace procrastination instead of improving your skills. Your future is based on the steps that you take now. Procrastinating could cause you to avoid some task that could bring about a considerable change in your life. Solving skill deficiency lies in identifying what those challenges are. Once you discover where the problem lies, acting towards correcting it will be easy.

Realizing That the Task Requires Hard Work

It is challenging to work on long and complicated projects because they require a lot of effort to be completed successfully. Sometimes, there are missed opportunities, and sometimes you may be forced to give up something that you like so that you can handle your project. This can make you lose motivation and even put aside your plans until a later time.

Most people value their personal time more than they value their goals or even their money. Some tasks will require patience for you to see results. For instance, many people fail in business because it involves a lot of effort and consistency. The few people that know this secret take steps to remain focused without procrastinating in order to achieve their goals.

Fear of Being at The Top

Getting Things Done and Stop Wasting Time

It may sound strange at first, but one of the reasons that people procrastinate is because they fear that, when they succeed, they will be in the spotlight. In this situation, the procrastination is due to the consequences that you will experience once you succeed. It is true that many people want to succeed and be at the top, but for some people, it is the reason that they are procrastinating. Do you find yourself dreading that if you perform well today, then people will be expecting even more from you the next time? Are you worried that your success will put you in the spotlight when you prefer a low-profile life? This point is talking about you.

People who experience this type of procrastination have an internal identity conflict. When your self-worth is determined by your performance, then it is easy for you to always challenge yourself to do better. What you don't realize is that with every success, you will have set yourself up for a bigger challenge. In time, this can make you lose your identity and have difficulties accepting your own success. At this point, taking no action or procrastinating may seem like the only way to avoid the pressure of trying to be good enough.

Chapter 2:
The Willingness to Accept Change

Do you always find yourself fighting change? This could be the reason you are procrastinating. The first step in overcoming procrastination is to accept change. It is not always easy to accept change, and it can require a lot of effort and determination. Our minds do not automatically embrace change, and it is something we struggle with all the time. For you to get over procrastination, you must be willing to step out of your comfort zone and allow some changes to happen in your life. The people unwilling to accept change have the hardest time, so having the willingness to change will help make things easier for you. When adopting the willingness to change as a way of overcoming procrastination you will need to do something more. You will let go of the old and allow new things to happen. You must accept that you have reached the limit in your endeavors and you must allow new things to take their place. Change is a life process, and you should embrace it despite not knowing what lies ahead. It lays the foundation to transform since it marks the beginning of what will happen in the future. Some of the things that you admire most occurred after some drastic changes took place.

Many people procrastinate because they fear the unknown. They are so afraid of change that they have no courage to take any steps at all. However, your willingness to accept change will make you embrace a new way of life. It gives you the preparedness to commit to new steps and face your fears. Procrastination tends to make us concentrate on only what we know, which limits our ability to take the necessary steps. By stepping out of our comfort zones, we will attain the inner growth that is necessary to overcome procrastination.

Willingness to change does not just entail saying or signing certain consent documents. It involves committing yourself to the important things in your life. There is no easy way to make the changes that you desire but reading this book will guide you in the following steps.

Ways to Accept Change

As said earlier, it is not easy to accept change, but for you to be able to overcome procrastination and enhance your growth, you will need to. It is true that you may not like how the world is transforming, but it is critical to adapt to these changes positively. Let us look below at the ways to accept change and overcome procrastination.

Accept Your Feelings Concerning Change

No matter what kind of change is making you uncomfortable, you need to embrace it. Ignoring your feelings concerning change will not help you overcome it. When you acknowledge your feelings, it will be easier to advance and avoid procrastinating. You can do this by expressing your feelings politely to other people. Failing to express your feelings may lead to bitterness and a negative mindset that can easily lead to procrastination. If you are dealing with grief or a sad and difficult situation, allow yourself to grieve. Holding onto grief for a long time will act against your moving forward. Don't allow your mind to remain in the past because you will be left behind. Embracing change is the very first step towards your journey to success.

Admit That Life Is Change

Change is constant and unavoidable, so you can do yourself a huge favor by accepting it. Many people procrastinate when faced with the reality that things must change. For example, your company may have introduced new procedures and processes, so being able to accept and adapt will help you avoid procrastination. Even before the time comes to make a change, you need to learn that changing old ways and things is essential in life. Everything that you see around you can be, in one way or another, attributed to change. Whether it is world history, developments, or administrations, all have resulted from people introducing and accepting change. Often, new opportunities come with change, and only those people who are willing to accept change benefit from such opportunities. The world is ever-changing and becomes very competitive, and therefore procrastinators have slim chances of achieving greatness. You should not set your mind and imagination in stone because this will make it very hard for you to accept reality. The reality is that change is inevitable.

Don't Allow Change to Control Your Emotions

People who are not willing to change tend to allow change to control their emotions. We all get overwhelmed by change at some point in our lives, but letting it control your feelings can be so harmful that it can make you procrastinate. Try to put things into perspective. You can do this by asking yourself questions concerning the change that you are facing and why it is upsetting you or making you fearful. Determine whether your thoughts are justified. Asking yourself some questions will help you have the right perspective about change. Ultimately, you will be placed in a good position to fight procrastination. You can adapt to change by looking back at the positive things in life. This will make you think positively and see beyond the perceived change. Most people see change as a door for bad things to happen and procrastinating becomes their only way to cope. However, this inhibits their ability to grow beyond their limits. Success comes by seeing beyond change, and you should not procrastinate when faced with a change in your life. Instead, refresh your mindset and embrace change.

Concentrate on The Brighter Side

It's true that change can be unpleasant, but procrastinating should not be the solution. Even in the worst circumstances, something positive can come out of it. You can turn the change that you are facing into an opportunity. For example, if you've lost your job, you should see that as a chance to look for a new, even better job, instead of opting to procrastinate. You can search for a new career or even find other ways that can sustain you. Procrastinators might not see these new opportunities. This may affect them in a huge way, and they may even find it very hard to find anything else to do. I have seen people who have remained stagnant without advancing for many years after losing their jobs. To them, change translates to an end. Having such a mindset is detrimental considering that we are in an ever-changing world. This is the problem of getting stuck in the same negative mindset. We may love our career or job, but in case something happens, and you lose your job, the best thing would be to find something else to do. It can be something completely different from your previous career or even another venture. This will not only help you avoid procrastination but also ensure that your life moves forward.

Know Why You Find It Hard to Accept Change

Knowing why you don't like change will significantly help you in handling it and even accept it. Think carefully and inwardly about it so that you can understand it well. This will help you eliminate the anxious feelings you have towards change. Procrastination is real, so knowing why change is so overwhelming to you will help you a great deal.

Why Do We Need to Accept Change to Avoid Procrastination?

Change will come whether you like it or not. The sooner you embrace the idea of change, the easier it will be for you to act. Our minds naturally embrace moments when only positive things are taking place around us. If it were possible, we would likely want to freeze time so that we could stay in that moment longer. However, when it comes to change, we fail to acknowledge it, and some people are so negatively affected by it that they procrastinate. We ignore the whole idea of change and fail to acknowledge that there could be anything positive that could come from change.

For you to be productive and avoid procrastination due to change, you must alter your mindset. Don't always assume that change results in negativity and destruction. Change simply means that things will not be the same again and will be handled differently. Look everywhere around you; would the world be where it is if there had been no change? Not. Due to change, we have cellphones, modern cars, computers, and many other amazing inventions and creations. The fact that you are reading this book on Amazon is as a result of change! In the past, for you to read a book, you had to visit a bookstore and buy it. However, through the many advancements in technology over the years, you can now simply upload a book from the internet and read it. So many opportunities have arisen after the world embraced change. Those who fail to embrace change by stubbornly maintaining their rigid mindsets are unable to benefit from the opportunities available.

The kind of mindset that you have will determine whether you will accept change or not. Learning to embrace change will give you the following lessons:

Reduce Your Expectations

Are you the kind of person who has high expectations for your family, your marriage, or even your business? The chances are high that you will become a victim of procrastination when things change. Having expectations that things will remain constant will seriously affect you if the opposite happens. Understand that nothing is forever. It is good to have hopes and expectations on how you would like things to happen, but don't be too rigid. If you don't have rigid expectations on your marriage or business, then when things turn out differently from what you had hoped, it will be easier to move forward. When you have high expectations and the opposite happens, moving forward will be hard, and you may start procrastinating on many things.

Embrace Change

Are you desperately trying to keep change from coming your way? You are not alone. However, learning to accept change will help you move forward even when the unexpected happens. Allow change to happen and try to determine why the transformation is happening. Understanding that not all circumstances will turn out the way we want them is paramount. When you accept the change, you will be able to adapt to the situation at hand, make the necessary steps to embrace it, and move ahead after the change. By doing this, you will rarely procrastinate.

Gain Knowledge from Experience

Accepting change will not only help you to avoid procrastination but will also teach you lessons. When you fail to accept changes in life, you may be distraught, things will seem meaningless, and procrastinating will be easy. Procrastination may be your mind's way of trying to avoid change. Reflecting on and accepting change will open the door to new knowledge that will help you keep pushing forward. You can learn so many lessons through change, but only when you open yourself up to them.

You Will Have Inner Peace

Permitting change and impermanence in your life will help you develop as a person. It will give you the strength that is required to take actions. When you proactively accept change into your life, you will be more calm, peaceful, and courageous. Once you realize that the twists and turns in life will not overcome you, it will be hard for you to fall victim to procrastination. You will be wiser in handling the changes in your life.

In the present era, you should not make change your enemy. Don't make it the reason for your procrastination. There are countless opportunities that come with change, but only the open-minded can take advantage of them. Instead of opting to procrastinate when faced with change, you should get out your comfort zone and act. After all, change can be good.

Chapter 3:
Dealing with Setbacks and Bad Habits

Setbacks and bad habits can make you procrastinate. You need to overcome them so that you can handle your most important tasks. Most people drag their feet on projects that don't attract their attention. However, ignoring a task does not make it disappear. Procrastination is one of the worst habits a person can get into because it limits your personal achievement. Procrastination has far-reaching effects in everything that we do. From procrastinating on going to the gym or putting off studying, the results will impact you and set you back from achieving your most important goals.

People procrastinate for various reasons. It can be due to being overwhelmed, lack of proper organization, or even lack of interest. However, in this chapter we shall explore how bad habits and your setbacks are making you procrastinate, and how you need to get over them. In the present world, it is essential to handle procrastination reasonably. If we fail to deal with it, serious setbacks can occur. Don't let your bad habits stand in the way of your success.

Getting Things Done and Stop Wasting Time

We all have our share of our bad habits, and no one can claim that they have none. However, some people experience habits that are worse than others. Some habits will cause you to procrastinate until the last minute when you start rushing. Some people are so badly affected by these setbacks that they lack the courage to step up.

The extent of your setback does not matter too much, if you are taking steps towards your dreams and goals. You should be willing to endure the occasional failure in order to achieve your goals. If your dreams and ambitions are backed by a strong reason or motivation, you will not view setbacks as working against you, but towards your success. Your ability to deal with setbacks will determine whether you will see them as defeat or as points to focus on to achieve your goals. The level at which you tolerate setbacks is proportionate to your willingness to get over them and take steps towards your achievement.

When you think about a current or recent setback that you faced, you will realize that setbacks reveal a lot concerning your character and can help you renew your commitment in your dreams. Instead of procrastinating when faced with setbacks and engaging yourself in less important issues, you should commit yourself towards your most important tasks. You should use setbacks to develop your determination to act towards your goals. The setback can be as big as the goal. When trying to achieve anything more important, you will need to apply more effort than if you are dealing with lesser tasks. Instead of being obsessed with our defeats or failures, we should learn the lessons that come with them.

Many people procrastinate because they wish tasks were more manageable than they are already are. But aren't there many people who have succeeded in every area of life? The answer is yes. Many people have succeeded even after making mistakes because they learned from their mistakes. Having a habit of looking for and taking on only easy tasks will be your setback and will make you procrastinate. Personally, I have gone through countless setbacks in both my personal and professional life. I was affected when I was unable to work on my weight. However, over time I have learned not to focus on the difficulties but focus instead on the lesson that you can learn from them. You need to develop a growth mindset instead of a fixed mindset. You may have experienced a point in your life when you no longer put much attention on failure after hitting a dead end. At this point, you will discover that your consciousness will change and having positive results will be easy. Your setbacks do not define your character but are a part of the process towards achieving your goals. This does not mean that you should not worry or care about your success and outcomes. It only means that setbacks should propel you further towards working on your goals instead of leading you to procrastination.

Don't allow your setbacks to affect your self-esteem. Instead, let them drive you to put in more effort. How we see ourselves when faced with setbacks will determine whether we procrastinate or whether we put more effort into achieving our dreams. Personally, setbacks have come as a blessing because they have helped me develop strength by exposing my weaknesses. This has helped me to become more resilient, and instead of wishing that things were much easier, I work towards making myself better. Wishing your tasks at hand were easier does nothing in helping you overcome them. Instead of procrastinating when faced with difficulty, we should increase our confidence so that we can always overcome. Note that the more you are willing to embrace setbacks, the more capable you will be in enduring defeat. Success involves going from failure to failure without losing hope or enthusiasm. You cannot have a life without any setbacks, so don't let them negatively impact your motivation, instead let them help you increase your efforts.

Instead of seeing setbacks as a sign of defeat, you can use them for your benefit. You will lose nothing if you remain focused on your goals. Any actions that you take have outcomes, and your success is dependent on those actions. If you choose to procrastinate because of past failures, you will lose your opportunity to achieve your goals. Procrastination will give you nothing apart from frustration and regret.

Ways to Overcome Setbacks and Procrastination
We all experience moments where, even after doing our best, we don't attain our goals. When you experience a setback, you can easily lose motivation and even opt to procrastinate. However, this can be avoided because there are proven ways to overcome setbacks, which we will discuss below.

Check Your Attitude

Always note that how you behave is influenced by your thinking. Therefore, when faced with a setback, instead of procrastinating, accept that you are going through a setback that you will ultimately overcome. Remind yourself of the setbacks that you've surmounted before, and that this one will be no different.

Make Changes

Instead of taking the risky step of procrastinating after a setback, alter some things in your daily routine. When you realize that a certain thing isn't working, try it a different way. Sometimes you will feel relieved by making certain changes. No matter how small the change is, it can significantly affect your thinking and motivation.

Be Flexible

When you are flexible in the way you approach things, you will know the changes that are needed in order to meet your goals. Lack of flexibility can easily make you procrastinate because you will find it hard to adapt to any unpleasant or unexpected obstacles in your life.

Seek Support

Sometimes you will need to find external support in order to overcome procrastination. Whatever you are going through, there is someone who has gone through it before and succeeded, so seeking their support will help you a lot. Procrastination is a real thing and handling it may require more than just yourself. In some cases, you will need to look for professional support. In any case, seeking support will cost you less as compared to what you could lose when you choose to procrastinate.

Be Positive

Being positive about your setbacks will not only give you peace, but also help you learn some life-changing lessons. When you are positive, it will be easier to avoid becoming a victim of procrastination. Procrastination is a product of negative thinking, and you can overcome it by being positive. Don't let your setbacks cause you to think that you can do your tasks later. The time is now because you never know what tomorrow will bring.

Be Confident

Even after going through setbacks, you should not allow your confidence to falter. In fact, it is in these moments that you should embrace your confidence. Even if you are tackling a challenging task, try to be as confident as possible. Most people procrastinate more on hard tasks than easy tasks. If you don't know how to handle a task, it is wiser to ask rather than waste time or delay yourself. Setbacks are real and happen to everyone, so you should not feel overwhelmed when faced with them. Don't beat yourself up during a setback; this will only worsen your situation.

After a setback, it is common for people to lose confidence and even procrastinate. However, you should use these setbacks to learn valuable lessons. Although perfectionism may seem like a good thing to most people, it can be detrimental to your success. Perfectionists often do not attempt things that they feel incapable of. To them, they can't accept a setback because they want perfect results. Stepping out and doing something will bring results; either you get what you expected or not. Either way, you can learn a lot from your actions.

Have Realistic Expectations

One of the reasons that you are faced with setbacks is because you have unrealistic expectations. Therefore, setting reasonable expectations will not only play an important role in overcoming setbacks but also in avoiding procrastination. Unrealistic expectations will only demand too much from you, which can easily lead you to putting your work aside.

After going through a setback, the least you can do for yourself is set reasonable goals. Unrealistic goals will only make you procrastinate and achieving anything will be a struggle. Identify the perfect place to start and make improvements later as you move ahead. This will help after a setback and help avoid another setback from happening.

If you are not careful, setbacks can hold you back and make it hard for you to advance. This can make you procrastinate over decisions and projects in both your personal life and professional life. Overcoming setbacks is essential in avoiding procrastination and achieving your goals. Don't allow your setbacks to pull you back; instead, understand the lessons they offer and apply them to your daily life.

Chapter 4:
Why Waiting for Tomorrow Is A Bad Idea

Think about how many things you have put aside and convinced yourself that you will do tomorrow! You have an assignment, but instead of doing it now, you are waiting for tomorrow. You tell yourself "tomorrow I will call my parents" or "tomorrow I will start going to the gym" or "tomorrow I will change my diet". To you, everything that you must do will get done tomorrow and not now. What you don't realize is that tomorrow will become today, and you might make the same excuse again. There is nothing special about tomorrow, and it will not magically make you act. Things will only get done if you decide that now is the moment to bring about change instead of postponing to tomorrow.

Think about today, was it not yesterday's tomorrow? It was, and there might be some things that you promised yourself that you would do. Have you done them? If not, you will agree with me that you should not befriend tomorrow. Stop wasting time by waiting for tomorrow in order to act. The only time you have power over is today.

When I was young, I had dreams. However, I told myself that I had to wait until I was 15 before I could start working towards them. What that did was cause me to wait for a time that I wasn't sure would come. What I did not know was that each day would come with its share of ideas and problems. Until now, there were some things that I regretted not doing at the time. In retrospect, I realize that I had the best opportunity then rather than now. Today, I have realized that time is moving very fast. From the moment I was born, time has never stopped, so I need to use that time well by working towards my goals.

Time is constant and does not wait for anybody, no matter how important you may be. It equalizes all people. Time gives opportunity but demands a sense of punctuality. Note that when your life is over, you will never have another opportunity to do the things you didn't do when you had the time. Whether you win or lose, time will continue to move. In fact, time couldn't care less about who succeeds or who fails. The only thing that will make the difference is how you spend your time, right now.

Don't Befriend Tomorrow

A friend of mine once told me that a person sees himself as three individuals: you in the past, you in the present, and you in the future. Although it is good to imagine our future self as more capable than both our past and present selves, you should not use that as an excuse to postpone everything until tomorrow. Does this sound familiar? You want to start exercising, but instead of starting immediately, you tell yourself that the perfect time to start will be Monday of next week so that you can start in peak form. Your mind tells you that starting in the middle of the week won't be as good because you should start on a fresh week. We are so involved in the calendar that we forget to realize it is we who determine our success and not the day. Your mind will tell you that your future self will be more focused, competent, and capable to deal with the task at hand. But how many can do what they said they would do tomorrow when it finally comes around? I can confidently say very few. This is because if people did what they promised they would do; the world would be full of successful and happy people. However, that is not the case. Many people think that they will be able to do later what they cannot do today. What they don't realize is that when tomorrow comes, the only thing that will have changed is time, and they are still the same with the same qualifications and capabilities. That is why you find yourself with a pile of things to do because you wasted your time by thinking that you would do them tomorrow. The bitter truth is that if your present self is not willing to do it, your future self will not do it either. No magic will transform you overnight into a better or more capable person.

If You Aren't Happy Today, You Won't Be Tomorrow

If you want to be happy tomorrow, you should start today. There is no point in convincing yourself that you will be happy tomorrow if you are not happy today. This might sound crazy, but when you look at it closely, you will realize that when your mind is focused on the negatives, it will impact your happiness. No matter what comes, it is probable that you will go back to these thoughts. Your perception of life, your focuses, and your thoughts will determine your measure of happiness, not your current situation. Therefore, stop waiting for tomorrow so that you can be happy; start now by focusing on the positives despite what you are going through. Many people are happy today even though they are going through tough times. Their secret is what they focus on – the positives.

If You Aren't Productive Today, You Won't Be Tomorrow

This means that sleeping today and waking up tomorrow will not change who you are. If you cannot accomplish that project today, what makes you think that you will finish it tomorrow? Your choices today will play a huge role in the type of habits you will have tomorrow. When you put things off today, you will have set yourself up for procrastination. When tomorrow comes, you may opt to procrastinate yet again.

We all go through situations that tempt us to push things off until tomorrow, but we should not give in. Maybe you have an assignment to complete and a television show that you want to watch. Part of you may want to finish the job before starting to watch the show, while the other part may convince you that since tomorrow you don't have a show to watch, you should just put off the assignment until tomorrow. Don't give in to the voices telling you to push off your assignment until tomorrow. When tomorrow comes, you will want to push the assignment off to the following day. This will make you unproductive not just today but also tomorrow, and if you don't ultimately change, your whole life will be unproductive.

No matter your age, you should have a drive that should push you to act now. The only moment we have control of is this moment, and we should use it wisely. Be cautious of the value of each day in your life. It's true that we might have all the time we need in the future – the next minute, the next hour, tomorrow, the next week – but if we lack a sense of urgency, we will not benefit from the available time. If you want to be productive tomorrow, you must start today. There is no point in thinking that you will spend your time tomorrow wisely if all that you are doing today is procrastinating.

Avoid Diving Too Far into The Future, Just Start

One of the biggest challenges for most people is to get started. That is why you are procrastinating and waiting for a day that will never come. The only thing that is standing between you and your success is the first step, and the best time to begin is now, not tomorrow. Just believe that today you have all that it takes to make a significant impact on this planet. Don't make a mistake that many others make – diving too far into the future that they ignore the present moment. Overthinking something could result in ending the idea before it has even started.

You can do this by having simple plans that you can start implementing right now with what you have. One of the reasons you find yourself waiting for tomorrow is because you have created overcomplicated plans. This can easily lead to procrastination.

Why You Must Start Today and Not Tomorrow

Your dreams must not be pushed off for tomorrow. Here is why:

Tomorrow Is Not Guaranteed

I fear death, and so do you, but the truth is that all of us are going to die someday. No one knows when. That means all you have is today and you should use it to at least start working on your dreams. You need to start avoiding that bad habit, start that business, or start exercising. You should start today. Don't wait for tomorrow because tomorrow is not guaranteed. Today is all you can be sure of, so make use of it.

Taking the First Step Will Determine How Your Goals Unfold

You can dream about anything, but if no action accompanies your dream, you will never see results. Everything that you see around you was a dream at the beginning, but it exists now because a person or group of people acted. If Karl Benz just dreamed about a car and never took a step to make one, we may never have had practical automobiles. In fact, he could have died without anyone ever knowing of his idea. When you have a dream, make your first step today, and you will be in the process of achieving your goals.

You Are the Change That the World Is Waiting For

You might think that you have nothing to offer. However, the world is yearning for you to take the steps that will bring the required changes. By taking steps today and doing something, you could bring about immeasurable change in the world that no one else could. Again, don't wait for tomorrow. Everyone is unique in his or her own way and taking steps today will mean that you are revealing your uniqueness to the world. Imagine if those people who brought immense changes and developments to the communication industry had procrastinated. Maybe you wouldn't be holding that smartphone or tablet right now. However, because they took those steps and didn't wait, there you have it – a lovely smartphone. Don't deny the world of your gifts and abilities by procrastinating. Once you figure out where your capabilities are, don't hesitate even for a day; start today.

You Will Open Immense Doors of Possibilities

Once you stop putting things off for tomorrow and doing them today, you will be amazed at how many doors of possibilities will come into view. Imagine that you are the boss of your own company and you have two employees. One does everything that you've asked right away, and the other usually tells you that they will do it later. When a new and better opportunity arises, who would you offer that opportunity? The reliable employee who does assignments promptly. No one wants to hear "I'll do it tomorrow" or "I'll do it later" in the real world. People want things done here and now. That is the mentality that you should have if you want to be successful. When you follow your dreams without delay, many opportunities will come your way.

Most doors will not open if all you do is sit down and wait for tomorrow. You will only see them once you act.

Take Charge of Your Happiness

When you do the things that you are supposed to do in a day, you will go to bed knowing that you have accomplished your goal or goals for the day. However, those who usually wait for tomorrow to act will not experience peace. Deep inside they know they could have done it if they didn't keep making excuses for themselves. Take charge of your happiness by avoiding procrastination and acting now, not tomorrow!

Begin Right Now

No matter what time it is, there is one thing you can do to start now and avoid falling victim to procrastination. When you open your mind, you will discover that there may be even one small step that you can take now. No matter how insignificant that step may seem, taking it now will give you an upper hand towards achieving your dreams.

Chapter 5:
The Power to Start (5 Second Rule)

You might agree with me that beginnings are always the most challenging part for many people. Whether it is the beginning of a small project or a large one, the challenge is still there. Maybe you want to start walking in the morning before starting your day's work, or you want to start working on your blog; the challenge will be the same. Regardless of how excited you may be or how much planning you've done, making that first step is scary. Many questions will come to mind: "Will I do it well?", "Do I have what it takes to bring this change into effect?", "What will people's reactions be?", and "Have I even made the right choice?"

Most of us experience this when we are starting a new year. You may have so many dreams and goals for the new year. When New Year's Eve comes around, we celebrate and party. We are full of hope that, when the new year begins, everything will go as planned. When January finally starts, we begin to question our ability to achieve our dreams. Instead of making that first step, our mind gets filled with so many "what ifs": "What if I start something and then fail?", "What if I am unable to do these things?", and "What if I lack the required energy to begin?"

When I think about the many books and essays that I have written throughout my career, I can attest that I started the same way. Any assignment that I was presented with took me time before I could start. I would question why I was doing it and stress that it was too difficult. The starting step is always the toughest. Surprisingly, when I finally started these projects, I no longer experienced those hardships.

I know I am not alone; you have also experienced the same thing when starting something. You might want to get in the habit of exercising. It might not be easy when first start, but if you push through and don't quit before you start, you will be so proud that you made that first step. Most people that I have talked to have admitted to putting off starting to exercise for several months or even years. Some finally did start, but others never started until now. Even those who have been exercising for many years will admit that waking up early in the morning and beginning the workout is always the hardest part. However, once you start, whether it's raining or sunny, you will get into the groove and even wonder why it was ever challenging to begin.

Why Are You Stuck to Begin?

There are many things that can make you feel challenged to start. However, fear is the number one reason why you get stuck before starting. When you fear failure in whatever you want to do, it will make it difficult to start it. In fact, when you give fear too much power and control, your mind will tend to focus on the potential failures and negatives, and you will likely procrastinate. No one is perfect, and we all fail at some point in our lives. Therefore, don't take failure too seriously. Even if you start something and fail, it is better than if you did not start at all because you will have learned something. Don't be a perfectionist. Believe in possibilities and see yourself achieving your goals after taking the necessary steps. When you are positive, you will do all that is necessary to achieve your dreams, but if you are negative, you will not even have the courage to start.

Being stuck at the starting point has far-reaching effect. It will prevent you from fully achieving anything in your life. The changes that you could make in the world remain untouched, and you don't develop. It is true that most people are not comfortable when starting, but don't allow that discomfort to deny you of all your opportunities. Face your fears head on so that you will not be stuck. It may be scary, but you will be amazed that after you have started, you will quickly gain momentum and see pleasing results. Whether you want to start a new lifestyle, or even a new store, just start. If you feel stranded, the 5 second rule outlined below can help you:

What Is The 5 Second Rule and How Does It Work?

The 5 second rule simply states that if you have the instinct to do something, you must move physically within five seconds or your brain will eliminate it. If people were honest, they would confess to procrastinating on some occasions in their life. Some people procrastinate because they have a lot on their hands, or they are trying to choose the task that requires the least effort. However, there is a type of

Getting Things Done and Stop Wasting Time

procrastination that is deliberate and negatively impacts both your personal life and professional life. Procrastination is a habit which we get into and effort is required to overcome it. However, all is not lost. If you apply the 5 second rule, you will be amazed at how you will get things done.

The 5 second rule was created by Mel Robbins in 2009 to help her overcome the habit of snoozing the alarm when it went off in the morning. It works like magic and can make it possible for you to entirely change any part of your life. First, let's provide an example. Imagine you are sitting near a swimming pool when suddenly you see a child in distress in the pool. There are no lifeguards around, it's only you, and there is very little time to save the child's life. You don't have much time to act. In such a case you will step into the water and help the child without even sizing up the risks. The fascinating thing about the kind of decision-making based on impulse is that it is based on deep science. Research conducted on human decision shows that emotional decision-making is just as important as rational or analytical decision-making.

Snap decisions like helping a drowning child are driven by a very quick-thinking part of your brain. Sometimes people say that this is acting on their gut, but it is also a way that evolution has adapted to speed up a slow and ineffective decision-making process.

The 5 second rule can help you improve any area of your life. If you need more confidence, more motivation, or help managing your doubts, you can rely on the 5 second rule.

When your instincts get fired up or you are sure you need to act, but you are feeling hesitant, this is the time to use the 5 second rule. You only have 5 seconds. You can do this by counting backward, 5-4-3-2-1, and then act. If you fail to act within those 5 seconds, chances are your brain will eliminate the idea and you will convince yourself not to do it.

Life is determined by 5 second decisions. Do you move to act or do you let fear take control? Do you begin to work on your decisions, or do you overthink and paralyze yourself? Do you talk about your concerns or do you remain nervous and silent? It all comes down to 5 second decisions.

5 Second Decisions

Within 5 seconds, self-doubt can take over and make your mind work against you. Therefore, you should move faster if you want to commit to anything. Therefore the 5 second rule is so important in changing your game. The moment you begin to count backward, you are interrupting your overthinking habit, you gain control, and you focus on taking new actions and easily activating other parts of your brain.

It may sound silly to count down from 5, but it remains a powerful tool of metacognition. This is a trick you can apply when you want to win over your brain and attain your dreams. You can use it to fully wake up from your inactive mode, interrupt your self-damaging habits, outshine your brain, and take charge of your life with only 5 second decisions.

Although it may appear simple, this act of counting backward, 5-4-3-2-1, has amazing effects on your brain. Habit researchers describe it as a 'starting ritual' that is responsible for triggering new positive habits. Mel Robbins says that, in her experience, the 5 second rule changes everything.

In 5 seconds, you can decide whether to eat healthily or unhealthily.

In a meeting, you can count down and decide whether to speak or to keep quiet.

You can decide to talk to an attractive person or see yourself as unworthy and let them pass.

The decision that you make in those 5 seconds will determine how your life will unfold in the future. Imagine how many opportunities you have lost just because you didn't make a move within 5 seconds. How long have you lived in your head thinking about the things that could make your life better? You have dreams but acting is a nightmare. You want to exercise, look for employment, share your ideas and opinions, and do anything that is important to your life, but acting on your thoughts seems impossible.

Some people think that by only thinking about the change, they will change anything, but that isn't true. The only thing that can change you is if you act. You will only see improvements if you try. Think about the many times you have told yourself: "This can wait", "I am not ready", or "I will do it the following day". We all procrastinate at some point, take too long to think, worry, and even doubt ourselves. It is a habit that can last many years if not handled appropriately.

The 5 second rule will teach you to stop concentrating on your worries and instead take steps that will change your life in a positive way. You can change your life one 5 second decision at a time. Although you can't always have the final say on your feelings, you have the power to decide to make a move. You will build confidence and momentum as you continue to apply this rule. This will continuously give you the outcomes that you desire.

Mel Robbins shared this rule for the first time on a TEDx stage and it has since risen to be among the top 20 TEDx talks globally. With over 13 million views and heard by over 100,000 people in over 80 countries, it is a simple idea with immense, immeasurable power. When you have an instinct to do something, you must move physically within 5 seconds or your brain will eliminate the idea. This means that when you have a goal of increasing your presence in the workplace, you just must count down from 5 and share the idea in your mind. If you are aiming to lose weight, count down and follow your set reminder prompting you to head to the gym.

The Elements of the 5 Second Rule

Let us look at the 5 elements of the 5 Second Rule and how each element is essential:

First: "The Time You Experience an Instinct..."

It is important that you understand the kind of instinct we are talking about here. An instinct does not involve buying everyone a drink in the restaurant. Neither is it a rash, irreversible choice; it isn't a harmful or destructive habit. The instinct that we are dealing with here is an urge, pull, or awareness of what you should do and what you should not because there is a feeling in your heart and gut.

These refer to the instincts of your heart. It is the time when your heart talks to you. Everyone has their own special brand of wisdom, resulting from experiences, intuition, and DNA. Within those 5 seconds, this wisdom fires up in you. This instinct causes your urges. They know that you ought to do something even if you aren't feeling up to it.

Second: "Acting on A Goal..."

This is an important element of the rule because it helps you understand that you are not to act on just any instinct, but only on the instinct that relates to a positive goal. For instance, your instinct might tell you to wake up early so that you can walk while going to work. In this scenario, if you obey your instinct, you will be headed towards improving your health. Though most people do not value instincts, research shows that the human 'gut instinct' is our 'alternative mind'. Usually, this gut instinct comes when both our heart and mind are trying to pass some information to us. In most cases, our gut instinct is connected to more significant goals.

People find it easy to list what they want: a good job, financial stability, happiness, or an amazing relationship. However, despite listing these goals, it is easy to avoid taking actions that would lead you to achieving these goals. That is why you should obey your gut instinct. If your gut tells you that you should call your grandmother, go ahead and do it because you are already aware of how valuable your grandmother is to you. If you are in a meeting and your gut instinct tells to raise some concerns, you should do it. You should do the same when you have an instinct connected to a goal.

Sometimes it is hard to understand where you should begin when working toward your goal. People have different goals, from getting in shape, having a good relationship, becoming happier, or even getting their dream job. The secret to achieving those goals is to identify the gut instincts that would attract you to your goals. You will discover that gut feelings are linked to your goals. The question is how to act on them. Find the answer to that question in the element below.

Third: "Push Yourself…"
Our minds are not always set to act, and therefore, you must push yourself. This means that, even if you don't like it, you should power through. This will help you take charge of your life one step at a time. This isn't

going to be easy. You must get out of your comfort zone and stop doing the same old things that you are used to doing if you want to change your life.

When you feel that an instinct is connected to a goal, you should know that there is a door of opportunity. Your brain will try to eliminate it. However, at this time, you can take charge because you are aware of what to do. You are aware that you need to change your life and head towards your goals. Although the 5 second rule appears simple, it is not easy to apply. No one likes the idea of pushing themselves out of their comfort zone. However, if you need change, you have no alternative, and the rule will help you. Just count down, 5-4-3-2-1, and go!

Fourth: "Move Within Five Seconds..."

The key is to physically move within 5 seconds. However, this does not literally mean jumping up and down; it only means acting according to your instincts. Always remember that if you fail to act within 5 seconds, your brain will eliminate the opportunity.

This can be anything, from saying something that you have kept silent about for too long, to raising an issue at a meeting, to eating that healthy snack, to applying for your dream job, or whatever else your goal may be. You can also use the rule to eliminate some of your bad habits like holding your tongue to avoid offending someone with your honest words.

Those 5 seconds can mean the difference between you transforming your life and your brain stopping you. You may be asking why 5 seconds and not 4, 8, or any other number? 5 seconds represents a thumb rule which can apply to almost everyone. However, this does not mean that you cannot personalize it. The idea is to minimize the time between the initial instinct and the time you make the first move. You can even do 2 or 3 seconds. Always keep in mind that there is a system inside you working at lightning speed to kill your dreams.

Fifth: "…Or Your Brain Will Eliminate It."

If you don't take a physical move within 5 seconds, your mind will eliminate your chance to take that opportunity. Your brain acts like a very protective parent. It thinks that by killing your instincts it is offering you protection, but it is stopping you from personal development, growing in business, and enjoying life to the fullest. Therefore, applying the rule will allow you to avoid procrastination and make moves within 5 seconds that will transform your life entirely.

Chapter 6:
Eat That Frog

We all have different tasks to do in a day. Some are tougher while others are a bit easier. It is normal for your brain to try and focus on the easier things first, but in this chapter, we shall show why you need to 'eat the frog' first thing in the morning. The 'frog' here refers to the tough task that you are supposed to accomplish. If you take the frog in the morning, there is nothing worse that you are bound to face during the rest of your day. This means that instead of starting with easier tasks like looking at emails or browsing through the internet, you should work on the most challenging task first. For instance, if your most challenging task is doing exercises in the morning, you should make all effort to do that before engaging in your other tasks. This will give you the satisfaction that you will probably not face a worse task than that during the day. Surprisingly, after you do the most challenging tasks, although you will meet other unpleasant tasks during the day, you will have the motivation to deal with them because in your mind you know you have already accomplished the most challenging task.

You may be wondering what you should do if you have more than one frog. The idea is the same. Though they are all important, they pose different levels of challenges for you. When you have two or more important things that you must handle, you should begin with the biggest, toughest, and the most important thing. To avoid procrastination, you must discipline yourself to begin immediately and be persistent until you are done with the task before committing to another task.

Many times, we procrastinate on the most distasteful things. You don't necessarily have to hate doing them, but maybe any time you want to commit to doing them, you find yourself looking for other things to do. You look for distractions instead of staying focused and getting things to happen. The funny thing is that these things have the potential to bring about a considerable amount of change in your life if you stop procrastinating on them. That is why you need to get into the habit of doing these things first, when you have the most mental capability and can better your situation.

Your frog will move your life in line to your desired future. Sometimes you may feel that your frog can wait, but it is advisable to eat it first thing in the morning when you have plenty of energy and willpower. Handling your most important task first is very important. When you wait, you will experience decision fatigue that negatively impacts your willpower and reduces your productivity. You may agree with me that you are not better placed to make a good decision in the evening because you are exhausted due to energy depletion. Even more of a reason that you should finish your most important task first thing in the morning when you have the most mental focus to handle it.

Additionally, during the first hours of the day is when you experience the least distractions. You should commit to doing your important tasks in the morning before anything else takes your attention. Whether it is at home or in your office, you will experience distractions during the day. The day usually gets crazy with many people and tasks demanding your attention, so handling your frog in the morning will ensure that they are not affected negatively during the day. It is probable that if you need to chat with a friend, you will not do it at 5 or 6 in the morning. You will wait until late in the day to talk to them. In the same way, you will not experience distractions from people very early in the morning, and so you should use this time to handle your most essential tasks. When you experience minimal distractions, you will be more focused and deliver even better results. I have read about many successful businesspeople who wake early in the morning and apply this principle towards building successful companies. Most of them get up early and start working because they know that all their competitors are asleep. You should act on your desire or your dream at the start of your day. You should eat your frog first thing if you are determined to experience growth.

How Do You Spot Your Frog?

Do you always have some tasks that you want to remove from your to-do list immediately? You also feel that if those were accomplished you would feel better, but you don't have the motivation to do them. It is possible that you push these tasks until the end of the day when you plan to tackle them, only to realize that you lack enough time to do them and probably push them to the to-do list of the following day. This can cause a lot of pressure and stress. In fact, those tasks will weigh heavily on your mind, and as time passes, they will become even heavier and prevent you from accomplishing anything tangible during your day. For you to have a clear view of your tasks, divide your to-do list into 4 parts:

- Things you need to do, but you don't want to do them

- Things you need to do, and you do want to do them

- Things you don't need to do, but you do want to do them

- Things you don't need to do, and you don't want to do them

Your frog will be number 1, the things you need to do, but you don't want to do them.

If You Have Two Frogs, Eat the Ugliest One First

If you have more than one such thing in one day, the simplest thing to do is to handle the biggest and toughest one first. When you face the most challenging thing during the first hours of your day, chances are you will do it with a clear mind, in a quiet place, and with the strongest willpower. This will be the best setting to handle the tasks that you don't want to do. Note that you should not wait long before eating your frog because you may get more tired, and it will demand a lot of willpower for you to tackle it.

Don't Sit and Look at Your Frog for Long

The secret to attaining high levels of performance and productivity is developing the long-term habit of handling your most important things the very first thing in the morning. Learn to create a habit of 'eating your frog' before committing yourself to doing something else and avoid taking too much time to think about it. This is a skill that has been used by many successful individuals, and it is essential for any person who hopes to achieve great things.

Take Immediate Action

If you want to be an effective and successful person, you must launch into your most important tasks directly and discipline yourself to work single-mindedly until you have completed them. Many organizations and individuals are experiencing failure in the execution process today. Many people confuse activity with achievement. Therefore, you find people continually talking and holding endless meetings where good plans and deliberations are made, but their talk is never backed by actions. With this kind of approach, it is difficult to see the required results. No matter what you dream, be it expanding your business, furthering your career, or impacting the lives of other people, if you don't change from just desiring goals to acting on them, you will never achieve any of them. When you have a dream, the best thing you can do is to act immediately. Having dreams will not give you any benefits or rewards until you take those necessary actions. You should act on your thoughts, set your goals, and learn to do what you need to do. You should act smoothly on any idea that comes into your mind. Always remember to begin with the task that will make you more productive.

Develop A Positive Addiction

It is possible to be positively addicted to endorphins and to the confidence, enhanced clarity, and competence that are triggered when you get the most important things done. For instance, when you start exercising, your body will experience pains and aches. However, after doing it for some time, you will crave the endorphins, and you will realize that your muscles allow you to exercise more efficiently and for a longer time.

You can also gain an addiction to achieving your goals while enjoying the path that you use to get there. Use this type of addiction to set your life in a manner that will help you start to complete important things on a regular basis.

Don't Look for Shortcuts

The key to mastering any skill is to practice. The best thing about our mind is that it acts like a muscle; the more you use it, the more it will grow. When you practice any behavior or habit that you desire or consider necessary, your mind will get used to it.

Common Objections When Eating Your Frog

Now that you know that the secret is to work on your significant tasks the first thing in the morning, let us look at some common challenges that people face when they are eating their frogs.

Challenges with Working on It Consistently

This a common struggle for most people, but the secret to overcoming this is to break down your tasks further. Note that this is your most important task and not your most important project. For instance, when you decide to write a full chapter in the morning, you may find the task too overwhelming, and you may end up writing nothing the entire morning. However, you have an option to break your task down further and then handle one small bit in the morning. By breaking it down into small achievable tasks, it will be easier to act without many obstacles. Through this, a process called solar flaring will be activated, which will make it easier for you to overcome your procrastination in eating your frog.

Being Unsure of The Most Important Task and Getting Nothing Done

You are likely to experience this if you are unsure about what tasks are most important. When experiencing this, all your tasks will appear important, and you may easily find yourself jumping back and forth amongst them. This will only leave you with many uncompleted tasks which ultimately reduces your productivity.

You can solve this by setting a goal framework in which you will determine your most important tasks. Have a chart that will help you decide which tasks are most important, or even which tasks are acting against your progress on some of your projects. You can do this by asking yourself one question – what is a single thing you can do that will make other things easier or unnecessary? When you put in place a framework to measure your success, you will not have difficulty answering this question. Also, have a habit of planning ahead as this will help you to handle your daily tasks with ease.

Challenges with Starting to Eat Your Frog

This is understandable especially if you don't like the task ahead. But remember, although you don't like doing it, it is necessary that you do it. Therefore, you should not waste your time just looking at the frog that you will have to eat in the end. Sitting for too long and thinking about the task you must do will only demotivate you. You should act right away, and when you experience some progress, you will gain the momentum that will make it easy for you to remain consistent.

Eating your frog means handling things that you don't enjoy doing. Your frog is your unpleasant task. The secret to eating your frog is to identify it and then act on it as fast as possible. It is true that you will have more than one frog on your list, but you must pick the ugliest frog first and eat it. This will help you face the day knowing that you've tackled the most challenging task and doing other things will be much easier.

Chapter 7:
Stop Filling the Void with Meaningless Tasks

How many times have you heard your colleague say how busy they are? How many times have you attributed your inability to do a task to your being too busy? In modern society, our worth, and that of the people around us, is measured by how much we can achieve with our time. It is a competitive world, and the only way to outdo one another is be productive with our time.

Podcaster and author Darius Foroux say that he got the same response when he asked his colleagues how they were doing – busy. This is the problem with most people – they think that being busy is being successful. However, there is as much of a difference between being busy and being successful as there is between day and night. What you may not know is that the kinds of words that you use when responding to people are aligned with your ideas. If you believe you are busy, you might as well act that way. You become efficient when you accomplish many tasks, but you will be effective when you succeed in doing the right things.

Do you know that you may be engaging in meaningless tasks right now, accomplishing nothing of value and only wasting your time? If you find yourself asking "why am I doing this?" or "is there anything of value in this?" then there is a high possibility that you are stuck doing some meaningless tasks that offer little to no value to your life and career.

Meaningless work refers to engagements that keep you busy but contribute nothing, and in the end, there are no satisfactory accomplishments. It often comprises of busy work that does not satisfy and is of little importance to you or anybody else. Most often, people engage in meaningless tasks because they are afraid of being idle. It is a way to prevent other people from having the idea that you are lazy. It is a form of gaining social acceptance and respect through constantly being busy or having a lot of work.

Instead of engaging in meaningless work, you should do meaningful work that brings results. Don't hesitate to question why you are participating in certain activities. Ask yourself how your work is contributing to the process of making a profit in your company. Is the work that you are doing adding something valuable to the world? Do you experience a sense of personal accomplishment when you do that work?

Being Busy Vs. Being Effective

Have you ever experienced this feeling?

You spent your entire day going back and forth – answering emails, completing your to-do list, attending meetings – but when the day comes to an end, you discover that you have accomplished nothing. You have done nothing on the list of your most important things; your workload is increasing until you reach a point where you question your productivity. The answer to this lies in the fact that there is a huge difference between being busy and being effective. You can never be productive by accident. It is an outcome of commitment to excellence, good planning, and being focused on your efforts. You should understand that you only have the energy for your work, for your relationships, and for yourself, and you should carefully guard it. This simply means that being busy will not automatically result in being productive. In fact, you could be wasting your time and energy on meaningless tasks, or have your time used up by distractions.

Get Things Done

Not all activity brings productivity. Productivity comes as a result of hard work, efficiency, and focus. Being focused means avoiding distractions as much as possible. This will help you stay committed to working for long hours so that you can push yourself and get things done. Most successful people have applied this idea.

A good example is Bill Gates who, at only 19 years-old, won the contract to develop Altair 8800 software. But how did he become successful? He set up camp in an empty room in a lonely hallway. The room had only concrete floors, some folding chairs, and a table with computers. While in isolation, he wrote the codes together with his partner, Paul Allen.

This does not mean that you always must push yourself to the corner or to isolation. What it does mean is that there is a time in your life when you must be completely and fully focused for a certain period, but it is a moment that will make a huge difference in your life. This is a practice that is employed by many great achievers when they make discoveries or inventions that bring about significant breakthroughs in their lives.

The reality is that there will be moments in your life when you will find the need to isolate yourself so that you can get things done. Doing this will significantly reduce all distractions and help you get things done. You won't just be busy.

Why Is It That Some People Work for Long Hours and Still Don't Get Things Done?

It is possible that you are working for long hours, but you are not getting ahead. Have you ever asked yourself why? Here are just a few pointers:

Distractions

People cannot work effectively with distractions from their phones – buzzing, incoming text messages, emails, and notifications from social media. When you allow distractions to get in the way of your important tasks, you will barely achieve anything. A distraction can be anything that prevents you from being committed and focused on your goals. It can be that little chat you are having with your colleague, browsing through the internet, or any task that you have clung to even though you know that it is not productive.

Interruptions

Your colleagues and family members can be a source of disruption, and at the end of the day, you will realize you have not done anything. It is very difficult to work when people keep asking question after question or keep coming to tell you stories throughout the day. Interruptions can lead to the loss of many hours of productive work in a day. Consider what you could achieve if all the time that you lost through distractions is added to your productivity. You will realize that interruptions are costing you a lot.

Lack of Proper Systems

Think about the many things that you do each day. If you lack the proper systems to do them, they can take more time than expected. When you lack a plan or a system that works, some tasks will occupy your entire day, making you feel like you have been incredibly busy when your achievement is insignificant. Most people confuse running around and being busy with being productive. Some even think that successful individuals often work for long, hard hours each day so that they can run their companies and projects, but this is not always true. What they do is work efficiently and productively by staying focused on their goals and having a plan to get them done. They don't work around the clock every day because they have systems and processes put in place to help them run their operations smoothly and effectively.

Don't Just Work Hard, Work Productively

If you don't know whether you are being productive or only working hard, these few warning signs can help you determine that you are expending energy yet remaining unproductive:

- You feel worn out from working the whole day, but you have not checked off anything on your to-do list.

- You frequently experience frustration, anger, and disappointment in yourself.

- You feel like you are being pulled in multiple directions, and you are unsure of how to get from one point to the next.

If you have been in any or all these situations before, you are not alone. In fact, there are many people out there who are experiencing the same thing as you are. However, your advantage is that you are reading this, and you are willing to take the right steps so that you can be a more productive and effective person. When you find ways to compartmentalize your time, you will get those crucial tasks done faster and more effectively. You will achieve this by minimizing your stress and having solid plans to do meaningful things with your time.

Ways to Eliminate Your Unnecessary Tasks

We often find ourselves doing repetitive tasks in our work because it seemed like the best idea when we started them. We continue to do those tasks, not because they are adding any value to our business, but because we committed ourselves to doing them.

Have you ever asked yourself why you are still doing them? The answer to this is because, as human beings, we tend to want to avoid losing things or giving things up. Let's use the clothes in your wardrobe as an example. Think about the clothes that you never wear, even though they seemed like the best purchase when you bought them. Why do you hang onto those clothes instead of giving them away, even after knowing that you don't intend to wear them ever again?

It is because you fear to lose. You've paid for them, so by holding them, you attribute false value to them. This is the same case with doing unnecessary tasks; it isn't because they add value to your work or business, but only because you were committed to them at the beginning. However, for you to be productive, you should let go of the unnecessary tasks that consume your time. The following tips will help:

Mark Your Most Important Tasks

Having a task list is not enough. You should be able to distinguish between your most important tasks and those that are just busy-work. Your high impact tasks are the ones that, once completed, will bring positive effects to your life. Note the three most important tasks for the day and commit yourself to doing them. Anything else should be done after those three are completed.

Exercise Saying 'No'

If you want to be totally free from being busy, you should learn how to say 'no' frequently. The only things that you should not say 'no' to are working towards achieving your goal for the day. When you exercise your right to say 'no,' you will be amazed at how much time you will have to focus on your major tasks.

Know Yourself

Knowing yourself better is the first step to stop being simply busy in your life. You can't have the courage to say 'no' if you don't know yourself. This means that it is important for you to know what you like, what you dislike, and what your capabilities are. Knowing these things about yourself will help you say 'no' to things that do not bring enjoyment to you. Always remember that joy comes from being able to do the things that matter the most to you. Before you commit your time to doing certain tasks, ask yourself the following questions: "What will I achieve?" and "What role will I play?" You cannot answer these questions if you lack self-awareness. This will significantly reduce the chances of being busy when you are achieving nothing.

Identify the Things That Keep You Busy

The first step in finding a solution is to know the cause of the problem. Ask yourself what keeps you busy. It may be emails, making phone calls, browsing the internet, and more. Sometimes you will need to track yourself for some days before identifying them. Once you identify them, it will be easy to overcome them. When you find you are wasting time through technology, certain apps and extensions, like Leech Block and

Stealth Kiwi, can help you block and avoid those technology time wasters.

Focus on Success

You should focus on the amount of time and hard work that you put into your personal or professional life. However, you can only succeed in this endeavor by ensuring that you eliminate all distractions. Eliminating your distractions means that you have removed anything that would otherwise work against your achieving great things. Always plan for your success because when you fail to plan, you have already failed. Accomplishing important things will absolutely need planning.

When you plan both your time and tasks, you will have uninterrupted time to get things done.

Put Your Smartphone Away

Is your phone keeping you busy? Then you should put it aside while working on your important tasks. You can do this by keeping it on silent or vibrate. Occasionally, you will be forced to place your phone in another room because some smartphones are loud enough that they can be heard from a distance even when vibrating. You may be worried about missing that very important call, but you most likely won't. You should plan your schedule so that you can work for the uninterrupted amount of time, followed by some short breaks where you can check for any missed calls.

Also, you can schedule a certain time of your day when you will return and receive calls. Recording a voicemail to relay that information to your callers will be helpful. This will allow anyone who calls you during your unscheduled time to know when they can expect you to call them back. This will significantly help you to remain undistracted when you are focused on your tasks, and make sure people aren't offended or discouraged when they cannot get ahold of you.

Chapter 8:
Your Environment Is Unproductive

We all go through this. Even when we have the intention of completing our task on time and as expected, we find ourselves facing distractions. Distractions can stem from a range of sources. They can be technological, environmental, or even human interruptions. How many times have you found that, no matter how busy you are, you still grab your phone when you hear a notification sound? You look at your emails frequently in fear that you might miss something. All of these are distractions which cause you to fail to meet your goal for the day.

Although you may think that you cannot avoid distractions, they can create a huge loss in your productivity. Statistics show that every 8 minutes, a typical manager is interrupted, and workers spend 28% of their time struggling with interruptions and trying to get back on track.

When performing your task, it is important that you give it your full attention. When you focus on a single task, your workflow remains constant and you can get more done within the set time. Also, focusing on a single task allows you to give that task the maximum attention and energy it requires, ensuring that you get the best possible results. Thus, it is important to eliminate as many distractions as possible. When you fail to avoid distractions, you will not be able to concentrate fully on your tasks. This will negatively impact the quality of your work. Thinking clearly will be increasingly difficult, and you will be prone to procrastination and wasting time. Most people are unaware of the amount of productivity they are losing to distractions. Anytime you fall victim to distraction, you are losing more time than just the amount of time the distraction takes up. This means that when you are distracted by a phone call for 10 minutes, you will not just lose the 10 minutes, but also the time it takes you afterwards to regain focus on what you were doing before.

Therefore, you should ruthlessly deal with distractions, but how?

Dealing with Environmental Distractions

Distraction is a real thing in our workplaces, and its effects on our productivity are real. Workers are distracted by emails, text messages, Instagram, Facebook and much more. Below you will find the common workplace distractions and how you can avoid them.

Noise

This may not apply to all workspaces, but those working in a shared office space are familiar with it. While it seems like a good idea to increase your interaction and share new ideas, sometimes it can lead to many distractions. Nowadays, most people are not using open office spaces due to one main reason – noise. Open offices have been known to be noisy and are not beneficial when doing work that requires a lot of focus and concentration. It is best for work that demands a lot of communication and collaboration. Therefore, you need to come with ways to prevent the noise from affecting you.

Not all people can afford to have a closed office space, especially those running new businesses. That is why you must come up with ways that can make the noise from an open office less impactful. One way you can solve this problem is to wear headphones. Just wearing headphones is a good signal to your colleagues that you are focused on something and don't want any distractions. When wearing headphones, you don't necessarily have to play music or anything else. You can just wear the headphones and not play anything. Some people prefer to play the music of their choice, or use white noise apps like Noisli, but others prefer just having the headphones on. You will be amazed when you realize that very few people will interrupt you when you have headphones on.

Smartphones

Nowadays, people are incredibly reliant on their smartphones. Smartphones are important in our daily lives since they allow us to stay more connected than we have ever been. However, if not used properly, they can be a major distraction.

A phone is the cause of distraction for most people more than any other device. You may not realize it yet but think about how much time you spend on your phone checking your social media or reading and sending text messages. In fact, this kind of distraction has to do with our brain. When you browse the internet, your brain releases dopamine, a chemical that makes you feel good and usually comes as a reward for completing tasks. However, the pleasure that comes from dopamine is fleeting, causing us to want to trigger the release of dopamine more and more frequently.

This is the reason you are constantly tempted to check your phone. Your phone triggers dopamine release, giving your brain temporary pleasure.

To fix this, you can silence all notifications during the time you need to concentrate fully. This is important because most of us depend on phones during business hours to make calls, so we cannot just turn them off. Some phones like the iPhone allow you to be on 'do not disturb' mode, which turns all notifications off. This will help you to remain focused at your desk without interruptions from your phone.

Interruptions

Interruptions are a common occurrence, especially in an open office layout where colleagues tend to frequently interrupt each other with questions and chitchat. When in such an environment, you can utilize a system that allows workers to signal each other when they are dealing with work that needs full concentration. You can have flags, signs, or even wear headphones to show that you don't want to be disturbed. You can also create an environment that encourages thoughtful communication and shows that everyone's time is important, which can lead to a big difference.

Clutter

Working at a messy desk causes more distraction to you than you realize. Your brain reacts to its environment, so when your workplace is cluttered, your mind will be cluttered, too. Remember that your mind is bound to wander if faced with challenging tasks. The best way to prevent your mind from wandering is exercising self-control, which can be challenging. Or, you can eliminate any distraction from your working environment, which is a much simpler step.

To fix your cluttered workspace, you can optimize your desk space to minimize distraction. Don't allow your attention to be taken by something else apart from the task in place. The first thing should be to clean your workspace. The key here is to minimize as many things as possible. Eliminate all clutter from your desk, and only leave behind the things that are essential to you while working.

Multitasking

We all make this mistake. You make calls when working or chat while reading articles. Though you think that you can manage two or three things at once, the truth is that our brains are not built to multitask. What you should understand is that anytime you are trying to multitask, you are intentionally distracting yourself from your most important tasks. In the end, you will realize that multitasking will prevent you from committing all your energy and focus to any one task.

However, this can be fixed by prioritizing. You must accept that your mind can only handle one task at a time. The question is, which one? You must prioritize and be careful when planning. Identify the activity with the highest importance or impact and commit to it with all your energy. You can also use task management software such as Asana that will help you set your priorities and track how you are progressing with your major tasks.

Emails

For most of us, the first thing we do in the morning is check our emails. We respond to queries, answer requests, and delete some junk mail. It doesn't end there; we leave our inbox open for the rest of the day, making it possible for us to see when a new email arrives immediately.

Sometimes, this isn't something we do intentionally. Most of us have been taught that immediately responding to emails is an important aspect of exhibiting our professionalism. This may be true to some extent, but when you look at it closely you will realize that your inbox can interfere with your productivity.

You can avoid this by designating times of the day that you will respond to emails. Start with your major tasks in the morning when your concentration level is high. After that, you can look at your email to see if there are any urgent messages. If there are, you can respond to them, but if there are none, you should continue working and respond to them at your designated time.

You might be surprised to realize that some of the emails that you thought were urgent weren't as important as you thought. And usually, any person who is in urgent need of you will find another way to contact you.

Though we can't remove distractions entirely, we can significantly minimize them by optimizing our working environment. The secret is to eliminate as many distractions as possible. Instead of immersing yourself in a daily struggle, the best thing is to remove as many distractions as you possibly can. This will help you remain focused on your major tasks and get more done.

Chapter 9:
Think Optimistically

When you are optimistic, you tend to see the best possible result in any situation. No matter what you are faced with, being optimistic will be important as you push to work harder towards the realization of your goals. Although most people will argue that they prefer to and try to be positive and not negative, many of them do not give it the attention it deserves. For some, positive thinking only remains on the surface. According to research, positive thinking is not just about being happy; it is a trait that, if embraced, can lead to added value in your life and can allow you to build skills.

The impact of optimism on your career, your health, and your life in general, is more than you could imagine. In this chapter, we shall look at the impacts of both positive and negative thinking and ways to increase positive thinking in your everyday life. Stay tuned and get enlightened.

The Impacts of Negative Thinking on Your Brain
Let us look at this example. Imagine that you are walking down the road and you suddenly see shooters in the direction that you are headed. In

this situation, your brain will register a negative emotion – fear. When you experience negative emotions, your mind is programmed to act in a certain way. When you see shooters before you, your instinct of self-preservation will kick in and you may think about running. Your focus will be on the gunmen and the fear that you are experiencing, and how you can escape it.

When experiencing negative emotions, your mind and thoughts will be narrowed and limited. Although there might be other options to escape from the gunmen, your brain will ignore all of them because they don't appear relevant when shooters are in your way. Your mind is programmed to react to negative emotions by limiting the outside world and the options that you see around you. Therefore, when arguing with someone, you might be consumed by your emotions and you fail to think about anything else. This is the same thing you go through when you are caught up in doing your task. Your mind may become paralyzed due to what is on your plate, and you won't have the time to do it. Or, when you are procrastinating, your mind might tell you that you don't have enough willpower, energy, or motivation. Because of this, it may seem easy to give in and not take any steps towards overcoming your situation.

In all these cases, your mind shuts out the outside world and focuses on the negative emotions that are going through you – fear, anger, or even stress. When you have negative thoughts, they prevent you from seeing other choices or options that are available.

The Impacts of Positive Thinking on Your Brain

Positive thinking helps expand your focus. It does this by opening your mind to see all the available options. For example, if your employee fails to deliver his assignment on time, instead of getting angry, you could use that energy to remind him to be professional and responsible. This will help you to experience joy, love, and contentment, which will allow you to see more possibilities in life. When you have positive emotions, your sense of possibility will be broad, and your mind will be open to many other options.

How Positive Thinking Impacts Your Skills

The benefits of positive thinking go beyond the good feeling that you experience for a short time. The most important advantage you will gain when you embrace positive thinking is an improvement of your ability to develop the skills and resources that you can use in your future. For example, a child who tends to run around and play with his friends may develop an athletic ability. He learns how to play and develops social skills to communicate with others. He also develops creative skills by exploring and examining the world that he lives in. Through this, the positive emotions of play allow the child to develop skills that are useful and helpful in his daily life.

The interesting thing is that the skills that this child will develop will go a lot farther than the emotions that led to them. After many years, the skills gained during childhood might develop into other beneficial opportunities. While the emotion that generated the creation of those skills might be already gone, the skills acquired will still be applicable.

This means that positive emotions and thinking expand your sense of possibilities and help open your mind, ultimately allowing you to develop new skills that can be beneficial in other areas of life. This is exactly the opposite of what negative thinking does. When you have negative thoughts, it will seem irrelevant to build skills for the future when you are faced with immediate threat or danger.

If having that positive outlook is so important in building valuable skills and changing the bigger picture of life, how do you get yourself to think more positively? Don't worry, your answer is right below.

How to Become Positive in Life?

Your mindset can make a situation good or bad. It is normal for a person to feel upset or angry when something goes terribly wrong. It seems natural to feel that way. However, this shouldn't always be the case. Research shows that the kind of happiness that you have is more of a choice than what is happening around you. How you view a situation will help determine how you will categorize it. While reacting negatively to a bad situation may be the most immediate response, we should not always embrace it.

Analyze Your Thoughts

In order to be a positive thinker, you must understand how to analyze your thinking. For example, when going through an unpleasant situation, try and analyze how your mind responds to what is taking place. Know whether you engage in negative self-talk, or if you mentally criticize yourself and other people. All these thoughts have far-reaching effects but identifying them is the first step towards avoiding them.

A lot of common negative thinking come as a result of concentrating so much on the unpleasant side of a situation. For instance, you may have spent a busy day at work and did almost everything according to plan. However, you forgot to make one important phone call. Despite all the success you experienced during the day, when you go home, your mind might only focus on that one phone call you didn't make. By focusing on the negative and only acknowledging your failure, you completely ignore the positives.

Avoid Self-Blame

Another common type of negative thinking is self-blame. It is common that when a company fails to hit its target, you might blame yourself for it. Instead, you should acknowledge that many aspects might have led to failures, such as the slowing economic growth and other internal and external factors. This can be so harmful to your psychological wellness. Taking the blame for things that you cannot control or are not your fault will lower your self-esteem.

Practice Meditation

Meditation allows you to display more positive emotions compared to people who do not meditate. Those who meditate develop long-term skills. They can exhibit mindfulness, live a purposeful life, increase social awareness, and lower their risk of illness.

Don't Be an Idealist

Many people think that positive thinkers only focus on the positive and ignore everything else, but for you to adopt this mindset effectively, you should train yourself to be a real optimist. If you fully ignore the negative, chances are high that you will harm yourself as well. Those who think positively can acknowledge both the negatives and the bright side, but they decide to focus both their time and energy to the side that will yield more positive results.

Have More Positive Friends

Bad occurrences greatly influence negative thinking. If you didn't already know, stress, happiness, and emotions in general are contagious. This implies that if you surround yourself with negative people, it is likely that you will start thinking negatively, too. On the other hand, if you surround yourself with positive-minded people, you will think positively, too. If you have decided to fully engage in positive thinking in all areas of your life, you should surround yourself with people who will help you in that direction.

Practice Gratitude

One of the ways I can shift my focus from negativity, disappointment, and judgment is to look back at the things for which I am grateful. This is a trick that I would like you to try because it can work for you, too.

Be grateful for the small things in life that you may take for granted. These can be things such as having a job, having a place to sleep each night, having people who appreciate you, or even having people that you yourself love and care for. As you exercise gratitude, you will immediately experience a major shift in your perspective. You can also keep a daily gratitude journal that will assist you in always remembering your blessings in your mind. Another good way to do this is to have a gratitude partner who can enhance your journey towards thinking positively. You can call, text, or talk to your partner about some of the things that you are grateful for. You will be accountable to this person in your journey to positive thinking.

Have Good Posture

Did you know that your posture can greatly affect how you feel and think? If you didn't, now you know. There is a great correlation between your mind and your body. This implies that when you stand up straight you will feel more confident than when you slouch. Having good posture not only impacts your mind, but also enhances the oxygen flow in your body. In addition, it reduces your levels of cortisol, a stress hormone, and improves the levels of testosterone, which improves your confidence.

The secret here is, if you find it challenging to put your mind into a positive perspective, then you should try and get your body there first. You can do this by standing up straight, keeping your shoulders back, holding your chin high, and stretching your arms as wide as you can.

You will realize that you will feel positive and more powerful. You will be amazed at how having good posture will help your mind be more positive.

Appreciate and Be Positive to Others

What you give to others will come back to you one way or another. It does not come from everyone or at every time, but what you give out matters a lot. What you send to people and how you treat them is the exact thing that you will get back. We often project our thoughts onto other people, so how you treat other people and the thoughts you have towards them tend to be the exact things you think about yourself. Therefore, as a way of promoting your positivity, you should offer appreciation and spread positivity.

One of the ways you can do this is by helping people out. For example, you can give your colleague a ride in your car, or if someone is looking for some information you can aid their search on the internet or ask a friend.

Also, offering a listening ear can be a great way of showing kindness and spreading positivity to other people. You might be surprised to know that sometimes people are not in need of a kind of direct help; maybe all they want is someone to listen to them when they voice their concerns.

Having positive thoughts does not mean that you should ignore reality and focus on your idealistic ideas; it involves taking a proactive approach in your life. Positive thinking allows you to handle life challenges by searching for ways that are effective in resolving conflict and having creative answers to challenges instead of being hopeless or overwhelmed. It may not be easy, but you will experience worthwhile positive effects on your emotions, your mind, and your physical health. It just takes practice.

Chapter 10:
Tunnel Vision Is Great

Tunnel vision is the tendency of some people to concentrate their attention on a limited or single objective or point of view.

Tunnel vision can also be defined as people looking at things from a very narrow point of view, not considering all the facts available. Having tunnel vision implies that you can achieve your goals, aspire to move towards them, and take risks to expand your boundaries in achieving those goal.

Tunnel vision causes individuals to have an opinion, limiting our ability to be open and see things. It helps us avoid getting stuck in the present and instead concentrate our efforts towards achieving our hopes and dreams.

Beyond Vision

Tunnel vision can also affect our hearing. There is a connection between the visual and auditory processors in our brain. As a human being, when you receive an audible message, it is processed by the auditory cortex, then packaged and relayed to the visual cortex. Here, they are converted to images. For example, maybe you have heard someone say "I see what you are saying" after you have given them a verbal explanation of something.

Double Duty
A vital part of our brain, the visual cortex, has two functions: processing information from the eyes, and processing audible messages from the ears. The problem is that the memory has a maximum capacity, and when it reaches its maximum level, some things must be given up. This depends on what thing that person is focusing his or her attention on.

Signs That You Have Tunnel Vision
Realizing that you have tunnel vision may be a bit difficult. The following signs are commonly experienced by those having tunnel vision:

- Irritated by people or things that are interrupting your focus
- Inflexible and unwilling to accept ideas and suggestions to change your plan of action
- Reluctant to take breaks from your work
- Confused or unaware of what is going on around you due to intense focus on a task
- Refuse assistance even though it could lighten the workload.

Importance of Tunnel Vision

Getting Things Done and Stop Wasting Time

For you to achieve your goals, it is always necessary to stay focused on your task. Staying focused is not a simple thing due to the multiple things that demand your attention and being overwhelmed by daily distractions.

Tunnel vision makes it possible for a human being to store the necessary information needed to achieve a specific goal. Our memory is limited and when we focus on many things, we end up forgetting important things. It is sometimes necessary to ignore information that you feel is not needed for you to achieve a given objective.

When you focus on one goal, fear is kept from inhibiting your action and achievement. Research shows that human beings experience fear of failure, and when you have many small goals, it can become too difficult to bear.

It has been noted we tend to focus more attention on the more important or challenging goals.

The Strategy of Focusing on One Task at A Time
It can be difficult to stay focused on one task, but it becomes even more challenging when you have constant distractions surrounding you, such as an urge to check your Facebook account or to catch your favorite show on TV. The ability to concentrate on one task is crucial as it helps you to achieve your goals, learn new things, and performing at your best in a variety of situations. Power to focus will have a significant impact on you, whether you succeed or fail.

The good thing with focus is that it is like a mental muscle; the more you practice, the more it builds up. It is possible to improve your mental acuity, but this does not imply that it is quick or easy.

The following tips will help you to be able to concentrate your focus on one task yielding better results.

Assess Your Mental Focus

Before you start working towards improving your focus, you need to determine how strong your mental focus is now.

You have good mental focus if:

- You can short breaks, and you get back to work immediately after
- You find it easy to stay alert
- You set goals by breaking larger goals into smaller parts

You need to work on your mental focus if:

- You are not able to avoid distractions
- You often daydream
- You lose track of your progress

If you find yourself experiencing the above, it is necessary for you to work on your focus. It will take some time, but if you practice standard habits, it will help.

Eliminate Distractions

Distractions can prevent you from concentrating on a task. Disturbances include intrusions such as noise in the background or a coworker stopping by to have a chat. Some distractions, like noise, are more easily minimized, but others, like an interrupting coworker, can be more of a challenge. To deal with such distractions, you need to take extra measures, such as requesting to have some time alone, or setting a specific place to complete your task away from distractions.

You must note that not all distractions are external. Some come from within, and they are difficult to avoid and ignore. Examples include anxiety, exhaustion, and poor motivation. You must come up with strategies to control these distractions. When you have positive thoughts, it ensures that you are well-prepared before you begin your task.

Live in The Moment

As human beings, it becomes difficult to stay focused when you are retracing your past mistakes, worrying about the future, or tuning out the present. Living in the moment involves setting aside all kinds of distractions, both your surrounding physical environment and your psychological anxieties. When you do so, you can become fully engaged in the current situation.

Living in the present is also crucial in improving your mental focus. This keeps your attention sharp and helps your mental resources home in on the details that matter now.

It is not possible to change the past, and the future is not here yet, but whatever you are doing today helps you avoid repeating past mistakes and helps pave the way for a prosperous future.

Take A Short Break While You Are Working

Maybe you have tried focusing on the same thing for an extended period. What did you notice? As human beings, our focus starts to break down after a while, and it becomes more and more difficult to commit our mental resources to that task. The result is that performance is greatly affected.

This happens because resources for attention are depleted, and it can arise due to the tendency of the brain to push aside sources of constant stimulation. It has been noted that taking short breaks, even by just shifting your mind to other things, can significantly improve your mental focus.

Practice Strengthening Your Focus

Improving your focus is not something that can happen overnight. To illustrate this, we may look at an example involving an athlete who is supposed to practice regularly to improve his or her performance by strengthening their concentration skills.

Start by recognizing the impact of what is being absorbed from your life. You should also start placing a high value on your time when you realize you are struggling to accomplish the goals by being distracted by unimportant details.

Multitasking

Multitasking is defined as the human ability to perform multiple tasks at the same time. It does not require the multiple tasks to be executed in tandem with one another, but it allows one task to advance over a given period. We are not able to do tasks at the same time; what we do is referred to as task switching.

For instance, a person may be reading an article, but at the same time, he or she is listening to music.

When the person is multitasking, his or her focus and concentration are significantly reduced. When this happens, it affects the person's performance, thus yielding poor results.

Effects of Multitasking on A Person's Focus

When you task switch, the tasks take more time to be completed compared to when you do each of them one at a time. You need a constant reminder of what to do next. This is a challenge to people, especially in web development and design, and in most cases not much work gets done; the individual is constantly worried about the next thing to do. This generally results in low daily productivity.

Task switching causes our brain to be distracted, and there is more of a possibility of making errors as compared to when you tackle one task at a time. This mainly happens when jobs are complete, and our brain finds it difficult to switch the tasks. This may affect your productivity by up to 40% per day.

Task switching activities involve the utilization of four major areas of your brain. The prefrontal cortex is used in shifting and focusing attention and selecting which tasks should be undertaken first. The posterior parietal cortex is involved in activating the rules for each task you are switching to, while the anterior cingulate cortex makes note of any errors. Finally, the premotor cortex prepares you to move and act. Research shows that people who are heavy multitaskers are poor at differentiating irrelevant information and relevant information because their brains have become less efficient and effective.

It has also been noted that participating in multiple tasks lead to diminished focus. For instance, in the case of an employee assigned several tasks, he or she will produce work which is of poorer quality than someone who was given just one task.

Ways to Minimize the Negative Consequences of Multitasking

Multitasking can have a great impact on our brain, thus affecting our performance, and those effects can be reduced using the following methods:

We should limit the number of tasks we are undertaking at any given time and should avoid handling more than two tasks at once.

Another technique of minimizing is referred to as the 20-minute rule. It states that human beings should try to devote their full attention to one task for at least a 20-minute period instead of constantly switching tasks. This has been known to have a great impact on our productivity as we concentrate our focus on one job at a time.

Chapter 11:
Kaizen to Overcome Laziness

Everybody, including me and you, are guilty of laziness. Many people have given up on their goals, both big and small, by just putting them off for next time – tomorrow, next week, or next month.

Generally, kaizen is applied to measure and implement continuous improvement. It is an approach that is based on common sense, order, economy, and self-discipline. Kaizen is a strong contributor and a motivator that helps people to reduce laziness in their working environment.

Kaizen refers to any tasks that continually improve all business processes, and it involves all employees in all lines of operations.

With the kaizen approach, the main priority is given to the manufacturing operations, as the process of achieving a result is no less than the result.

The history of kaizen began soon after the Second World War when Toyota first implemented quality circles in their production process.

Getting Things Done and Stop Wasting Time

This was necessitated partially by American businesses and some management teachers who visited Japan.

A quality circle is a group of employees performing similar tasks who meet regularly to identify and solve work-related problems. The kaizen approach became very popular in Japan, and it has continued to exist in the form of kaizen groups.

In the modern world, the kaizen concept is designed to address issues over the course of a week, and it is referred to as a kaizen event. This event is focused on a development project that is intended to accomplish breakthrough improvements in a short duration.

Are you aware of why most people set goals, but then fail to accomplish them? Most of them try to set goals and objectives, but, unfortunately, they end up failing to accomplish their plans.

Many people start when they feel very strong and confident, but along the way, they become weak and frustrated. In the beginning, they are determined to achieve their goals. Along the way, they lose their steam and motivation, and they end up getting distracted by the busyness of their lives. Due to that, they find themselves procrastinating, and their laziness kicks in, only to end up with them giving up on their goals.

Kaizen is a powerful technique that you can apply to overcome this challenge and get rid of laziness.

Remember that the main reason most people fail to achieve their goals is because they try to achieve too much within too short a duration of time.

In the modern world, most people want to get rich and become successful as quickly as possible. They forget that doing so requires tireless efforts to break old habits.

Note that a habit can be very difficult to change, especially negative habits that are deeply ingrained in you. Therefore, if you are trying to achieve something within a short duration of time, then you will end up suffering from a drastic habit change. This is not a good technique to use to achieve what you may want in life.

Most of the people around the world are unable to cope with some drastic habit change. This is because their bodies are not used to coping with the change. They end up feeling tired, lazy, unable to concentrate, and unable to perform even though they have more time to do some tasks.

This is the major reason why most people around the world find it more difficult to achieve what they have set out to do. Eventually, they end up choosing to procrastinate, and they let their laziness take over their lives. You should not let this happen to you.

Getting Things Done and Stop Wasting Time

Kaizen is a simple and powerful technique that you can use to overcome laziness, and it helps you accomplish things within a short duration of time.

Kaizen, also known as a 1-minute principle, is a modern technique that has been used by many leaders in managing their businesses in Japan.

The technique allows people to cope with change very slowly and very wisely. This implies that, when you want to achieve what you desire in life, you need to act on it very slowly and very wisely, not spontaneously.

The technique is based on a 1-minute principle for gradual improvement. This suggests that, if you want to achieve something, you need to practice it every day at the same time for at least 1 minute.

It is extremely vital since anyone can do something for only 1 minute a day. But most people tend to think that this technique is not effective, and many are doubtful since they believe that people can only achieve success by putting in lots of time and effort.

Contrary to that, when you try to put in more effort over a huge chunk of time, you will end up getting exhausted very quickly. Ideally, this is not the best way to start any task or any goal.

In addition to that, when applying this technique, you will have to break down your major goals into smaller chunks of actionable steps since this technique will require you to work on the task or goal for just 1 minute.

This technique is perfect because it turns your big goals into smaller, more manageable steps that you can perform each day. Most importantly, the kaizen technique allows you to see your progress; thus, it ends up motivating you. You will be able to see whether you are achieving your goals or if you are still lacking in time.

For most people, acting on your goals for just 1 minute per day will not be a big issue at all. Note that you need to start doing whatever you plan to do in just 1 minute. Whether you are writing a book, writing a simple article, or reading a book, start doing it for just 1 minute a day.

The moment you perform that task in 1 minute, you will be able to watch your progress, and you will experience a sense of success and victory. This will end up motivating you to move forward.

1 minute of action will become 5 minutes, 5 minutes will evolve to 20 minutes, and so on.

The key to the kaizen technique is to start small and then grow slowly. People often try to tackle and achieve their goals through performing everything all at once, and they end up failing. You should not fall into this trap.

You can easily achieve your goals, live your dreams, and accomplish whatever you want to in life. However, you must first understand what goals you want to achieve in life and then do them for just 1 minute per day. In other words, apply the kaizen technique and start small expecting to grow big.

When you do a task for just 1 minute per day, it will take you little energy, and it will not require too much motivation. I am sure you can do it if it is just for 1 minute per day. In addition to that, you will be able to see yourself making some progress, and you will start seeing small victories. This will help you to reduce laziness, boost your motivation, and encourage you to keep moving forward.

The kaizen technique will also help you develop the right behavior or habit that you need to achieve success in whatever you are doing.

Some kinds of change need a major project which means many months of continuous hard work and big budgets. However, an alternative approach to improve processes and systems is through ongoing changes and continuous improvements.

Kaizen - A Great Technique to Overcome Procrastination

Often you set new goals, and you end up failing to achieve them. You end up convincing yourself that you are not ready, and you end up giving up easily. You may be trying to achieve your goals too quickly. When you fail to achieve your goals, you quickly get tired and bored, and you end up procrastinating.

Kaizen is a great technique that will help you to overcome procrastination and reduce laziness. The technique takes just 1 minute, and the results are impressive.

This technique is perfect, and anyone can apply it in their sphere of life. The technique advises people not to change their life spontaneously or suddenly, but wisely and slowly. The new habit should come as a result of reflection and life experience.

Why Is It a Perfect Technique?

In the beginning, this technique might seem ineffective, people doubt it because they believe that they can only achieve their goals through tireless efforts. That is not the case. Some challenging tasks of self-improvement that require a lot of energy may end up exhausting you and end up leaving no tangible results.

Whatever you are doing, the task will not seem like something unpleasant that you must manage. Instead, it will become a task that brings you joy and satisfaction. Therefore, take just one little step at a time, and in the end, you will find yourself moving down the path of self-perfection.

The kaizen technique lets you see the small steps of progress you are making, and it is a critical part of forming new habits.

It is vital for you to overcome that lack of confidence that you might have in your abilities and free yourself from helplessness and guilt. To move forward with your achievements and success, you need to experience a sense of victory.

When those feelings of victory start inspiring you, you will gradually begin to increase the amount of time you spend on the goals that you have set for yourself.

You need to determine the goals that you want to achieve and start doing them for just 1 minute every single day.

As we have seen earlier in this chapter, the kaizen technique is based on the idea of a 1-minute principle. You should practice doing something for 1 minute every day at the same time.

This is something manageable because even the laziest person can afford to do it. Maybe in the past, you have made excuses for delaying longer tasks, but in this technique, we are only talking about doing a task for 1 minute a day. I am not telling you to do it for 30 minutes or 1 hour, but only 1 minute a day.

Whether it is your new working routine, or some other goal, when you are performing it for only 1 minute a day, then the task does not seem as difficult, and you will not make any excuses.

Therefore, use and apply the Japanese kaizen technique to whatever you are doing, and you will see how it will help you to overcome laziness and change your life forever.

Chapter 12:
There Is No Shame in Rewarding Yourself

Everyone likes a pat on the back after accomplishing something. There is no better time to get one than when you are out of your comfort zone and challenging yourself to improve; you may even be nervous about whether you are going to succeed.

A lot of people approach changing their habits from the perspective of the plan. You will find them constantly nagging themselves, berating themselves, and expecting nothing but perfection, despite how much progress they make.

To some people, beating themselves up may seem like the best way to get motivated. To motivate yourself, try to approach your objectives and goals from the perspective of possibilities. You need to find some way of rewarding yourself and encouraging yourself. Instead of concentrating on something that you did wrong, pay more attention to what you have done right.

Rewards tend to help you feel that you are doing something that you want to do, and not just what you are forcing yourself to do. Note that even the smallest and minute rewards can work wonders and make a difference as you move from milestone to milestone.

To develop a good reward system, you need to do the following:

Choose Some Benchmarks and Reward Levels: In this step, you need to reward yourself for levels of consistency. After you have chosen your benchmarks and reward levels, make the reward meaningful to you. Make it as relevant as possible.

Come Up with Some Reward Options: This does not take much, and in most cases, the best rewards are those that you cannot buy. Note that a lot of small rewards that are used to meet smaller goals are more effective than relying on bigger rewards that will require more time, more work, and more energy.

Plan to Celebrate: You need to figure out how you are going to celebrate your small achievement. Involve and inform other people about your small achievement. You need to create a celebration that you are always able to anticipate and remember to keep it within your sight.

Be Honest with Yourself: Remember that mentally fudging the numbers will hurt your cause of building a habit that will last a lifetime. Note that keeping your focus on building a positive habit is not just figuring out how to get the reward.

Behavior that gets rewarded often gets repeated. For instance, tell your dog to sit and when it does, reward it with a treat. Do this a couple of times and your dog will quickly learn to sit when you tell it to.

This is how exactly how behavior works in human beings, and that is how habits are built as well. They always involve a cue, a response, and some rewards. Note that it is only when your brain starts anticipating a reward that the power of the habit fully kicks in.

This implies that rewards drive human behavior. Unrewarded behavior tends to die out while rewarding behaviors get repeated. That is the reason why this chapter has concentrated on the strategy of rewarding yourself to reduce procrastination. Therefore, continue reading this chapter and the whole book to teach yourself how you can procrastinate less by using behavioral psychology and the power of rewarding yourself.

Rewarding Yourself as A Strategy to Overcome Procrastination

To overcome procrastination, reward yourself for even the smallest achievements you have made. In other words, you need to praise any slight improvement you achieve.

Up to now, you may already overcome procrastination occasionally. In most cases, you have the willpower and the strength, and all that is remaining is to reinforce this behavior. From now on, when you overcome the urge to procrastinate and you get something done, you need to reward yourself. Reinforce the habit that you want to be repeated.

Generally, you can use the following tricks to reinforce your good behavior:

Practice Internal Self-Praise: When you find yourself doing something right, you should give yourself some internal self-praise to acknowledge that you have done something of worth. Do not just push it aside and assume that you have done nothing. Instead, take your time to acknowledge it and celebrate your good habit a little bit.

Keep A List of Accomplishments: In this step, you need to write down all your small wins no matter how tiny they may seem. This is to ensure that you acknowledge them and do not just forget about them.

Use A Reward Substitution: Many positive habits only reap rewards far in the future, making them unappealing for our instant gratification-seeking brains. Therefore, you need to substitute those long-term rewards with immediate rewards. When you perform a task successfully for about 45 minutes, consider rewarding yourself with something good. When you finish working on a certain project, then treat yourself. This will motivate you and help you reduce procrastination.

Ideally, the pleasant emotions that are generated by self-praise and other rewards tend to creep back into the effort itself. Note that by combining your efforts and rewards you will end up learning how to associate tasks or activities with something desirable.

What you must note is that these effort and reward cycles lead to a phenomenon known as learned industriousness. This means that getting rewarded for some efforts leads to higher efforts in the future. In other words, by rewarding yourself for your little efforts, you end up training yourself to exert higher efforts in the future. You associate your efforts with positive emotions and rewards.

Chapter 13:
Time Chunking Never Fails

The best method to manage your days, weeks, months, and even years is to use the time chunking method. You need to chunk your time daily. In this method, you will set aside certain chunks of the day for activities or tasks depending on the time you have at your disposal.

You can dedicate certain days to certain activities and tasks to allow yourself to keep that much further ahead of all that you have on your plate.

By switching to this method of chunking time, you will be able to see your tasks and projects better than before. This will allow you to make decisions to stop working on those tasks with more confidence since your time chunking process will show you what you had time for and what you did not.

Also, by time chunking your week rather than your day, you will have room for more flexibility. Whether you work from home or in an office, you can chunk time in the same manner, or you can use a combination of weekly and daily time chunking so that you can make better use of your work time.

When you decide to do time chunking, I will advise you to start chunking your time by day of the week. In this case, you need to choose certain days of the week to do certain activities or tasks. For instance, you may decide to make Monday the day that you will perform all your administrative activities. In that way, you will get the bulk of them done and have those responsibilities out of the way earlier in the week.

On Wednesday, you can set aside some time to work on an activity or a project that is going to be exciting. This will re-energize your body and give you the motivation that will carry you through the remaining days of the week.

Friday could be a great day for you to set some time chunks aside to reflect on how your week has been and take some time to prepare for the week ahead of you. From there, you can jump into the weekend with a clear mind and enjoy your time away from the office more fully and completely.

After you have gotten used to the idea of time chunking your weeks and your days, then you can consider breaking it down into hours of the day as well. In this case, you can use tools like 30/30 for iOS or Emergent Task Planner.

Getting Things Done and Stop Wasting Time

Time chunking will allow you to work with optimal productivity. It is worth trying in some form because it will remove a decision from the process of performing what task to perform and when to perform it.

Time chunking is a great strategy that will help you to define your time slots and help you tackle certain tasks throughout the day. The chunks are dedicated only to specific tasks. They can be as long or as short as you want, but they should be focused on a specific thing. This helps you avoid distractions.

Time chunking is a method for getting into the right zone. It helps you find your flow and allows you to truly focus your attention on the activities that you need to accomplish.

In many cases, people have fuzzy or vague ideas of what they need to do on a certain day. They may settle in to start an activity, maybe spend around 15 minutes on it, and then the worst thing happens – their attention shifts.

Maybe you receive an email or a phone call, maybe somebody stops by your desk, or maybe you end up remembering something else that needed to be accomplished. Whatever it is, you will end up shifting your attention and start multitasking.

Most activities we work on are normally accompanied by startup time. How much time this activity will take will depend on the task, but it is always there, and the worst thing you can do is to start multitasking.

The startup time will become a waste if you do not finish what you have already started. Note that you will have to go back to the drawing board again, which is an avoidable challenge if you utilize time chunking.

Chunking means that you know exactly what your objectives and goals are for the day. You know what to start and how long it will take you to perform a certain task. You, therefore, need to protect that time and prevent any obstacle from hindering you as you work on your project. You will focus on a single activity and finish it before moving to the next item on your to-do list.

In this modern world, people often feel as if they are being pulled in multiple directions with an endless list of activities to be performed. They feel like they never have enough time to do all those activities. Time chunking is the best solution to all these problems. It allows people to take control of their time and their work, which makes things more manageable.

The quality of your output is dependent on two things. The first thing is time. You should dedicate enough time to what you are doing. The second thing is a clear focus. By focus, we mean avoiding distractions, vague objectives, and aimless work habits.

This is where time chunking comes in. It will help you to focus as well as allow you to improve the quality of your work.

How to Chunk Your Time?

If used correctly, chunking can be a very powerful method. To unlock its value, you need to follow the following steps.

Update Your To-Do List

Note that to chunk your time effectively, you must first know what you are trying to accomplish. Often, people do not know what they need to get done or what is the most important. They settle in for work and throw themselves into their work without thinking or prioritizing.

Instead, take about 10-15 minutes and review what you have done and what you need to do in the next minute or the next day. Prepare yourself well for what is to come. The important part of this process is for you to be specific in your objectives, goals, activities, and tasks. The more specific you are, the better you can allocate your limited time wisely.

Designate A Time Slot for Each Task in Your Day

After you have come up with your to-do list for the day, you need to go ahead and assign each task a time slot indicating when you will be working on that activity. You can do this in several different ways, from the availability of time, to the priority of the activities. You need to take your best guess or estimate on how long each task will take and consider putting it into your schedule.

Note that chunking requires practice, too. You will be aware of how much time activities take along the way, so do not worry about getting it perfect the first time around. The activity may take 45 minutes or 3 hours, but that understanding will come with more experience.

The priority is to schedule your time chunks and then stick to them.

Turn Off the Distractions

Before you begin on any chunk of time, it is essential to eliminate all distractions in your way. You can remove those distractions by silencing your phone, shutting your office door, getting any beverage you may need, disconnecting from the internet if possible, or playing some music that will help you find your flow. Consider using headphones to drown out any noise that may distract you.

I believe that you know that you procrastinate, and you know how you get distracted. Therefore, taking the necessary measures to prevent the expected distractions from taking hold will take you a long way.

Perform the Task and Gather Data

What is now left is for you to perform the task. Note that for any chunk of time, you need to be focused on a single activity with your undivided attention.

Generally, you get that activity done, but either way, as that activity ends, you should assess how it went. Assess whether you had enough time to do it: did you did it to your best ability or did anything distract you? All this data and information can help inform your next session, and it will help you to improve your ability to chunk your time overall.

Time is the most valuable resource you have, and therefore you should manage it well. How you spend your time will determine who you become as a person.

If you wish to achieve your objectives and maximize your time, then chunking is a great way to achieve it.

Find Time to Chunk Your Tasks and Stop Procrastinating

Note that finding time to stop procrastinating is among the best time management skills that you can ever develop for yourself. But it is a challenge to most people.

It does not do you much good to allow your inner critic to try to goad you into an activity when you find yourself procrastinating. This may lead to increased stress and maybe the introduction of your inner rebel to that conversation. It is a fantastic recipe for digging your heels in deeper and coming to a virtual standstill.

Remember that you do not know that you are procrastinating unless you have some clear goals that you need to achieve. The good news is that if you know that you are stuck, it is because you know where you want to go and what you want to do.

Getting from where you are now to where you wish to go involves a lot of effort, and the effort is work. This implies that you must invest your time and energy. The moment you invest effort, you will expect to reap a good reward.

Therefore, in one way or another, the major source of procrastination can be the size of the gap between the investment in effort and the reward. If the gap is large, then you may face the challenge of procrastination.

If you have a big project to do, a project that is going to take many days, weeks, or even months to finish, then when will you start to see the benefits of your work? It will require some skills and discipline to get started on a project like that.

However, the advantage is that you can build your rewards. It is possible to do this by the way you structure your activities or tasks, the way you remind yourself about them, and what you tell yourself after completing each step.

Chunking these activities down into small manageable sizes is a key component of any attempt to overcome procrastination and focus on your goals. Note that chunking is a time management skill that may give you steppingstones and some stopping places that allow you to provide yourself with pats on the back along the way.

Ideally, what chunking does is reduce the gap between the effort and the reward. Therefore, when you find yourself procrastinating about something, grab a piece of paper and note down the activity at the top. Then, create about 15 steppingstones to get yourself to your goals.

Getting Things Done and Stop Wasting Time

Begin with a first, small step as soon as you have finished noting down your steppingstones. If you cannot do it immediately, be certain to schedule a specific time and then commit yourself to it.

Notice how your energy is changing, and the impossible begins to feel possible. Remember that chunking and creating some steppingstones are the key. Any time you invest your effort, be sure to validate yourself with some reward such as taking a break or treating yourself to something you enjoy.

Chapter 14:
Stop Sabotaging Yourself (Manage Procrastination)

Sometimes it is easy to sabotage yourself, especially when you are trying to meet an important goal such as saving money or getting assignments done. Self-sabotage is not a simple thing. It can have many causes, but the results are that you will end up getting off track and you will not get things done as expected. This can lead to feeling bad about yourself, and you may end up failing. This only leads to more self-sabotage, like procrastination, as you try to avoid facing failure.

Why Are You Sabotaging Yourself?
Note that there are many things that could lead to self-sabotage, but the most important ones involve your thinking patterns, your fears, and your tendency to avoid things that are very difficult to perform.

One big way you may sabotage yourself is by not dealing with challenges until they become too big to deal with. In other cases, you may not be able to discipline yourself enough to get tasks done on time.

There are many potential reasons why people procrastinate. For instance, you may have never learned some of the skills that may help

Getting Things Done and Stop Wasting Time

you break tasks up into smaller pieces, or you may be too tired to plan or schedule your activities.

You may be overwhelmed by the magnitude of the activity, or you may feel like you do not have what is required to succeed.

If your self-sabotage by remaining stagnant and not getting started, going out with your friends instead of working could be facilitating your procrastination. Note that in the short run, you will manage to avoid the discomfort of an anxiety-ridden and unrewarding task, but in the long run, all the things that you have put off will come back to bite you.

You may procrastinate because you can't decide when and where to begin. This tends to cause anxiety. You can overcome it by giving yourself a time frame or a time limit to select or allow yourself to make an imperfect choice. This will help you to learn something from the experience and eventually improve over time.

Procrastination can also prevent you from taking responsibility for your actions. This allows you to blame outside factors such as not having adequate time. Most people fear success because they shun the spotlight, or they fear that others will expect more from them than they can deliver.

With self-sabotage, one size does not fit all. Sometimes you may be too stressed and tired of thinking through complex choices, and instead, you end up relying on easy but inaccurate heuristics. For instance, you may sabotage a relationship because you fear rejection. Or you may end up procrastinating because you fear failure and you lack adequate time management skills.

Steps To Avoid Self-Sabotage

Understand Self-Sabotage

Most people are engaged in self-destructive behaviors that eventually become bad habits. They allow these behaviors to undermine the continuation of their success, but they may not even recognize that they are doing it.

Self-sabotage is when you do something that might end up getting in the way of your success or of your bigger goals and dreams. You want something, but somehow you never accomplish it because something deep in your subconscious is fighting against that goal.

In many cases, your subconscious may see self-sabotage as self-preservation or to safeguard yourself even when it is no longer needed.

Recognize Your Self-Sabotaging Habits

The major step to break up the cycle of self-sabotage is to become aware of your behaviors. Try and look at your behaviors from an objective point of view. Recognize what self-destructive behaviors, mindsets, and patterns are pulling you back.

In this case, procrastination occurs when, instead of handling important tasks promptly, you allow yourself to rush to complete it at the last minute. It becomes hard to succeed and shine when you do not give yourself enough time to fix mistakes and do a thorough job. Therefore, to work towards your goals, start by setting deadlines and milestones.

Take Time for Self-Reflection

You need to engage in some serious self-reflection to understand why you keep shooting yourself in the foot. Taking time to reflect on the issues you seem to be inflicting on yourself may lead to a deeper awareness and give you some insight into yourself and your underlying desires.

To avoid procrastination and succeed in whatever project you are doing, take the time to reflect on your choices, decisions, and actions. You need to learn from what has worked and what has failed, and then adjust your course of action by taking different approaches.

It is only through self-reflection that you can gain the necessary insight and understanding to begin the process of transformation.

Change Your Pattern of Behavior

Note that changing your negative behaviors is fundamental if you are to stop sabotaging yourself. In every moment, you are taking action that either moves you toward or away from the person you want to be and the life that you want to have. Those bad behaviors that you keep encouraging are the ones that will keep you from reaching what you desire.

Make Small but Meaningful Changes

To stop procrastinating, begin by making small but meaningful changes that you will slowly build to create larger transformations.

When you realize that you are sabotaging your success by continually and constantly missing deadlines, take one step back and look for a small but meaningful change that you can make to set you on a more successful track.

If, for instance, you are disorganized and constantly getting off track from what you are supposed to be doing, take about 10 minutes every morning to organize your office and write down your to-do list.

If you are constantly missing your deadlines, you need to sit down and come up with a reasonable timeframe to get your tasks done. From there, take the necessary steps to reach your goals. Ultimately, you will end up accomplishing your goals while still building your confidence.

Chapter 15:
7 Steps to Stop Procrastinating

Do you consider yourself to be a procrastinator? Many people around the world consider themselves chronic procrastinators. This suggest that they procrastinate in multiple different areas of their daily lives, including relationships, health, work, and finance, among other daily routines.

Procrastination is more of a time management issue than anything else, but often it is all about avoiding certain emotions. In some cases, you may procrastinate if the activity at hand seems pointless or boring.

In another case, it could be that you are too afraid of performing badly that you end up feeling paralyzed and you cannot even get started.

Note that most people who procrastinate tend to focus on the short-term benefits rather than the long-term benefits. For example, they get hung up thinking that the task is going to be too hard, they do not know how to do it, or it is going to be uncomfortable, instead of accomplishing it.

Even though you are procrastinating and trying to avoid whatever unpleasant experience you think you are going to have, by deciding to avoid it you will still have that activity hanging over your head and waiting for you. Therefore, it will still have a negative effect on you even if you are not actively doing it.

While procrastination is not a psychiatric diagnosis, it can still lead to stress, poor performance at school or work, and health issues.

Procrastination can negatively impact your relationships, both emotionally and physically.

However, this chapter brings you the good news. The good news is that it is possible to overcome the habit of procrastination. As you are aware, nobody was born with the habit of procrastinating and, therefore, you can break yourself out of this bad habit that you have learned.

Here are the major steps that will help you to stop procrastinating.

Admit Your Mistakes and Forgive Yourself for Procrastinating in The Past

Many people beat themselves up over their mistakes, and they think that they are too lazy to perform some tasks. However, considering yourself a procrastinator may make you procrastinate. Therefore, even if you have pushed off some projects in the past, you need to give yourself a short break and consider moving on.

You may ask yourself how to go about forgiving yourself. To forgive yourself you need to think about what happened in the past and ask yourself how you can improve or do better next time. If you do that, you will not dwell on the shame and guilt you feel. Instead, you will free up your mind, focus on solving problems, and get more tasks done.

If you forgive yourself, chances are you will not repeat the same mistakes in the future.

Be Honest About Your Priorities

How many times has someone asked you to perform some tasks, and you keep making the excuse that you do not have enough time to do it right at that moment?

People love to use lack of time as an excuse because it is easy. Remember that no one is going to accuse you of having too much time on your hands. When you make this excuse, you only end up hurting yourself.

Instead of doing that, it is better to be honest with yourself and others. Just tell the one giving you the task to perform that you appreciate the offer, but that task is not a priority for you right then. By doing that it will force you to confront the white lies that you often tell. It will help you to recognize what is important to you and what is not important.

Evaluate what is a priority for you. You can do this by keeping track of the goals you want to make for a certain duration. Record your goals with a Word document, paper and pen, Excel document, or anything else with which you are comfortable. Then, put them away and set a calendar notification for the last day of your recording period.

At the end of your recording period, go through your list and see which goals you have accomplished and which ones you did not manage to accomplish. From there you can decide whether to delete them, put them lower on the list of priorities, or do them.

Note that if you say that you will wake up every day at 5 a.m., but every morning you slap the snooze button until it is 7 a.m., then you are not going to wake up at 5 a.m.

If you claim that you are going to make your bed every morning, but you have huge tasks that you have not worked on in the last month, then you will find it hard or pointless to make your bed every morning when you remember that you have these crazy tasks at hand.

Therefore, it takes a lot of self-awareness to be honest about your weaknesses and strengths. By looking back at your past failures, you can end up changing your future for the better.

The best part about this strategy is that it stops that low level of anxiety that people get from having a bunch of goals bounce around in their heads. The moment you decide, you can live a guilt-free life and use your energy to commit to activities and tasks that you can perform.

Stop Feeling Guilty

Getting Things Done and Stop Wasting Time

It is surprising how many people fall into a spiral of guilt, and they do not even realize it is happening. How many times have you talked to your best friend about something like saving money, studying for school, or working out and their response is "I know that I should be doing that, but..."? They always give some lame excuse as to why they are procrastinating on doing something very important.

This is exactly what happens to people who are in credit card debt. Most of them do not even know how much debt they owe. They would rather avoid their credit statements than face the reality of their debt.

This happens because of guilt. It is the reason why people tend to brush things off with mere excuses and run away from the truth.

Therefore, if you want to stop procrastinating and become productive, then you must hold yourself accountable. You do not need to run away from your guilt.

When you feel guilty, follow the following steps to address it:

Acknowledge the guilt: The moment you realize that you are feeling guilty about something you are putting off, take a moment and acknowledge that feeling. You need to recognize your guilty and consider asking yourself what is making you feel guilty.

Use the "five whys" technique: A Japanese industrialist by the name of Sakichi Toyoda developed the "five whys" technique. The technique was aimed at finding solutions for the root of recurring issues that were related to his manufacturing firm.

At the bottom line of the technique is the question "why?" The idea of this technique is that most problems can be solved by asking yourself "why?" 5 times, sometimes even less than 5 times, and you get to the root issue.

Say, for instance, you feel guilty because you have been meaning to open a savings account, but you haven't yet. You can utilize this technique through something like the following example:

- Why do I feel guilty?

   I feel guilty because I have not opened a savings account.

- Why have I not opened a savings account?

   Because I do not know where to begin.

- Why do I not know where to begin?

   Well, I got a savings plan book 5 years ago, but I haven't even read it yet.

- Why have I not read it?

   Because it is in a box in my basement.

Getting Things Done and Stop Wasting Time

What you must have noted is that in less than 5 "why" questions we can figure out how we can start to solve the problem. You can solve a huge issue with just one step, that is, taking your time to find the book. In our example above, we now know that this person has the first step to getting started with his savings account project.

Note It All Down: You need to take everything from the above two steps – your guilt and the 'why' questions – and note it all down. This will help you get a clearer understanding of how your brain works when it comes to guilt and problem-solving.

Act: However, once you have noted everything down, step back and give it some space before jumping right in.

You cannot stop procrastinating by trying to do everything at once. This is because, as human beings, we have limited willpower.

Note that just performing the five "whys" and investigating your guilt takes a lot of energy. Therefore, step back and pick it up when you are fresh and ready to act. It is advisable that you set aside some time in a day or two so that you do not push it off.

However, next time you find yourself saying something like "I will get to it later" then you should stop and evaluate it.

In some cases, it may not be your priority now, or maybe you do not want to perform it. Both thoughts are fine. In doing that you will save a lot of time and effort by recognizing and acting on what is going on.

Build Systems to Accomplish Goals

How do you find motivation? There are a few insights from this question.

Motivation is undependable; if you wait for motivation to fall from nowhere so that you can accomplish your goal, you'll never achieve that goal. Build the right systems instead. This is a better approach to getting things done than just waiting for motivation to strike.

Therefore, instead of waiting to be inspired and motivated, you need to ask yourself what it will take to accomplish your goal.

This should not include higher-level concepts like teamwork or determination, but it should be about developing concrete steps that will allow you to get to your goals. This will assist you in developing a strong system that will help you to accomplish your goals. To achieve this, you should try breaking down your goals into smaller steps.

Tackle Your Most Important Task For 20 Minutes

Instead of wasting time thinking about the total number of hours you need to spend working, just start working. Encourage yourself by saying that you have only to perform the task for 20 minutes. This will help you to deal with the intimidation factor, and you will likely spend much longer than 20 minutes on your task before you stop working again.

Break Tasks Down into Smaller Chunks

Sometimes it can be a bit overwhelming to think about getting through an entire month's worth of activities. Instead of thinking about the large tasks that you must do, break them down into smaller tasks. In doing so, you will be able to get started on the smallest tasks and move forward from there.

Reward Yourself for Your Good Work

Note that rewarding yourself after a task well done will help you create a powerful shift in your mindset. For instance, eating a couple pieces of chocolate after an intense workout is a very simple step that may help you to ignite the reward centers in your memory and cement the fantastic feeling that is required for a habit to take root.

Sit down and ask yourself: what habits do you want to start, and how are you going to reward yourself for acting?

The True Facts About Procrastinating

For you to truly stop procrastinating, you must come to terms with the truths of productivity:

1st Truth: All of us have the same amount of time in a day, so you need to stop using time as an excuse. You need to learn how to manage your time.

2nd Truth: You do not have to be a robot to stop procrastinating. Time management and good focus are about positive mindsets and simple, yet powerful shifts on how you approach your tasks.

If you adopt the right mindset, you will create good habits instead of constantly struggling to get the simplest tasks done.

Chapter 16:
Stop Wasting Time on The Internet

Technology is focused on making people's lives better through convenience, automation, and instant gratification. However, due to these technological advancements, people have ended up procrastinating more than ever. Many activities and tasks that they used to do manually are now computerized and automated. These activities are being completed in a shorter amount of time, and with less effort.

While one major goal of technological advancement is aimed at giving people more time to perform more tasks and activities during the day, most people are not using it this way. Instead, they end up wasting more time instead of using it for the better. In other words, overuse of technology has led to the underutilization of our cognitive abilities.

Technological advancement is one of humanity's greatest accomplishments, but if it is used improperly, it can negatively affect our lives. Therefore, we must be wary about how we interact with technology.

You should not allow technology to dominate your life. Instead, you should see it as a tool that can make your life more convenient. If, for instance, you have an activity or a task that requires immediate attention, you need to recognize that and avoid being distracted by any technological gadgets. You need to focus on the activity at hand by turning off all your notifications – turn your phone off or put it on silent or vibrate mode.

There are billions of people who suffer from crippling procrastination, and it is a real drain on efficiency and productivity. Many people do not want to procrastinate; they would rather work to their full ability, but they cannot seem to avoid procrastinating.

Procrastination can be caused by different factors in different individuals. Some may procrastinate due to a lack of clear direction, while others might procrastinate due to exhaustion or a busy schedule.

When it comes to the internet, you need to look at what sites benefit you and which sites distract you. For instance, using social media, like Twitter and Facebook, too much can be very dangerous. You can lose both your concentration and valuable time, and you may end up becoming addicted to many unhelpful and unnecessary things. You can even end up losing control of yourself.

Take this scenario, for instance. When you are on Facebook and scrolling through the news feed, your brain makes thousands of decisions. These decisions may include whether you should pay attention to your friend's comment or photos, whether you should like and comment on their photos, or whether you should make a post of your own. You end up using more energy in making these decisions, and this may result in making poor decisions and, finally, procrastination.

You could end up making thousands of decisions in an hour. So, what will happen for the rest of the hours in the day when you are supposed to make important decisions? You will find that you do not have enough energy to make the most rational and effective decisions.

Internet kills someone's time faster than anything else. Within minutes you can watch your favorite episodes of your show, chat with your friends on Facebook, and watch the latest uploads on YouTube. It is like a never-ending rollercoaster of distractions.

What you fail to understand is that excessive internet surfing tends to function like any other addiction. It ends up hacking the reward system in the brain and makes you feel uncomfortable engaging in the real world of tasks and activities: exercising, working, socializing, and other things that are supposed to fuel your personal growth.

Internet addiction has a strong impact on depression, anxiety, and stress.

In order to stop wasting your precious time on the internet, you need to follow the following strategies.

Set Firm Boundaries for Online Work

You need to set a time frame for work only. For instance, you could work from 9-5. You can decide to have some free time before or after your set time frame. When you stick to this time frame, you will be developing a strong habit after two or three weeks, and later, it will become second nature.

If you find it too difficult, you can work in shorter durations of 30-45 minute. Don't check your usual distractions in between these stretches but allow yourself to walk around for a few minutes or get a glass of water before refocusing and going back to your workstation.

You could consider installing a timer on your computer and keeping it in front of you while you are working. The time will help remind you that you do not have time to waste.

In addition to using a timer, you can use online tools that can help you to stop wasting time browsing on the internet. Some of these tools include, but are not limited to, News Feed Eradicator and Leech Block. These tools can help you remain focused for as long as possible.

Take A Day Off from Technology

You are defined by more than the sites you browse. Therefore, consider going out on the weekend for the entire day. Take a walk with your best friends, or sit in a park reading novels, magazines, or books.

A lot of movement will create energy. Therefore, when you are out and about, you will end up attracting dynamic energy, things, and people into your life, and this will make you feel fulfilled and excited about the life that you have. As a result of that, you will not waste time browsing through the internet when you go back to your work computer.

Stagnation ends up attracting stagnation, and it blocks growth and rejuvenation. Therefore, browsing through the internet will stagnate your energy and make you live inside your head. Remember that you should not live inside your head for 6-10 hours a day, yet many people do exactly that.

Make the Internet Harder to Access

People tend to do what is more comfortable for them when they can do that. Therefore, you will find people pressing the snooze button or avoiding workouts multiple times a week.

Therefore, to take advantage of this little-known knowledge, make all online distractions harder to access. You can use blockers for all your social media, change your passwords, and consider putting your browsing gadgets, like phones and tablets, physically far away from you while you are working. This will help you to avoid wasting time and will help you concentrate on your important activities of the day.

In most homes, the Wi-Fi is turned on 24/7, which can lead to internet addiction. You can avoid this by making a habit of turning your Wi-Fi off for a set time frame in the evening hours. For instance, you do not need Wi-Fi 3 or 4 hours before going to bed. Consider spending those hours with your family members and close friends. This habit will increase the quality of your sleep, and in turn, you will increase your productivity.

Create A Life Outside of The Internet

The best strategy to remove bad things from your life is by adding good things instead. Therefore, if you want to get rid of internet surfing, add activities that will end up revitalizing your spirit.

There are so many activities that you can add to your life. You can spend time in the park, read interesting books, socialize with family members and friends, engage in your hobbies, exercise, write in your journal, and volunteer, among other helpful activities.

Build Your Self-Control with Small Commitments

Staying away from browsing through the internet is like fighting any other kind of temptation. However, when you have self-control and you are grounded inside yourself, you will not feel the need to drink, binge eat, or waste time browsing the internet in order to escape uncomfortable physical sensations and feelings.

For you to create strong self-control, you need to make small sacrifices and commitments. Limit how often you eat your favorite snacks. Take warm or cold showers instead of hot baths. Choose to stay away from the internet for about 45 minutes every evening. These small acts of mental toughness will end up building up your inner stability little by little.

Have A Work-Only Computer

If you have more than one computer, you can remove the temptation of browsing through the internet by dedicating one of your computers or laptops solely to work. Do not install applications such as social media clients or gaming platforms unless they are work-related.

For example, if you are using Chrome and you have Chrome sync enabled for your Google account, you can use a different Google account on your work computer so that your time-wasting bookmarks do not sync over. If you are not willing to do that, then hide the bookmarks bar.

It is even a good decision to use your work computer in a location other than where you use your leisure computer. Find a specific location that you like and use it as your workspace, but never use that same location to play computer games, for instance.

Tame Your Email Addiction

This is the worst habit among many people. The challenge is that emails never stop coming in. Some of these emails require careful, thought-out replies.

By frequently checking your email throughout the day, you are constantly switching your focus from one important thing to another, and you never give yourself enough time to fully focus on one thing.

The solution to that is to block out time for receiving emails during the day. You can dedicate one hour of the day to reply to emails, and all other hours are to be spent doing other things while your email notification tab is closed.

Track Your Productivity
What gets measured will get managed. If you consider tracking your productivity at your work computer, you may be surprised with what you find. During working hours, how much time do you spend doing the actual work, and how much time do you spend browsing the internet or idly chit-chatting instead?

Track all these activities and review the reports later. In most cases, you will find that you are less productive than what you expected.

Don't Browse Without Purpose
Many people tend to browse the internet without any purpose. You can find them right after work or school powering up their computers and idly browsing.

Here's my advice to you: avoid doing that. Do not do it to unwind or to see what is new on the internet. Always have a purpose when browsing the internet.

If you find this book helpful in anyway a review to support my endeavors is much appreciated.

Getting Things Done and Stop Wasting Time

Paul B. Heathcote

www.ingramcontent.com/pod-product-compliance
Lightning Source LLC
Chambersburg PA
CBHW031119080526
44587CB00011B/1030